ART BOOKS

FROM CRESCENT MOON PUBLISHING

Leonardo da Vinci
by James Pearson

Early Netherlandish Painting
by Rosalind Mutter

Piero della Francesca
by Naomi Haskell

Giovanni Bellini
by Julia Davis

Eric Gill: Nuptials of God
by Anthony Hoyland

Minimal Art and Artists In the 1960s and After
by Laura Garrard

Postwar Art
by George Knighton

Vincent van Gogh: Visionary Landscapes
by Stuart Morris

Max Beckmann
by Stuart Morris

Egon Schiele: Sex and Death in Purple Stockings
by D. Simon Eade

Mark Rothko: The Art of Transcendence
by Julia Davis

Jasper Johns
by L.M. Poole

Brice Marden
by Laura Garrard

Frank Stella: American Abstract Artist
by James Pearson

The Light Eternal: J.M.W. Turner
by Jeremy Mark Robinson

Maurice Sendak and the Art of Children's Book Illustration
by L.M. Poole

Sex in Art: Pornography and Pleasure in Painting and Sculpture
by Cassidy Hughes

Glorification: Religious Abstraction
In Renaissance and 20th Century Painting
by Jeremy Mark Robinson

The Art of Andy Goldsworthy
by William Malpas

Andy Goldsworthy: Touching Nature
by William Malpas

Andy Goldsworthy In Close-Up
by William Malpas

The Art of Richard Long
by William Malpas

Constantin Brancusi: Sculpting the Essence of Things
by James Pearson

Alison Wilding: The Embrace of Sculpture
by Susan Quinnell

The Erotic Object: Sexuality in Sculpture
From Prehistory to the Present Day
by Susan Quinnell

Land Art: A Complete Guide to Landscape, Environmental,
Earthworks, Nature, Sculpture and Installation Art
by William Malpas

Land Art In Close-Up
by William Malpas

Colourfield Painting: Minimal, Cool, Hard Edge, Serial
and Post-Painterly Abstract Art From the Sixties to the Present
by Laura Garrard

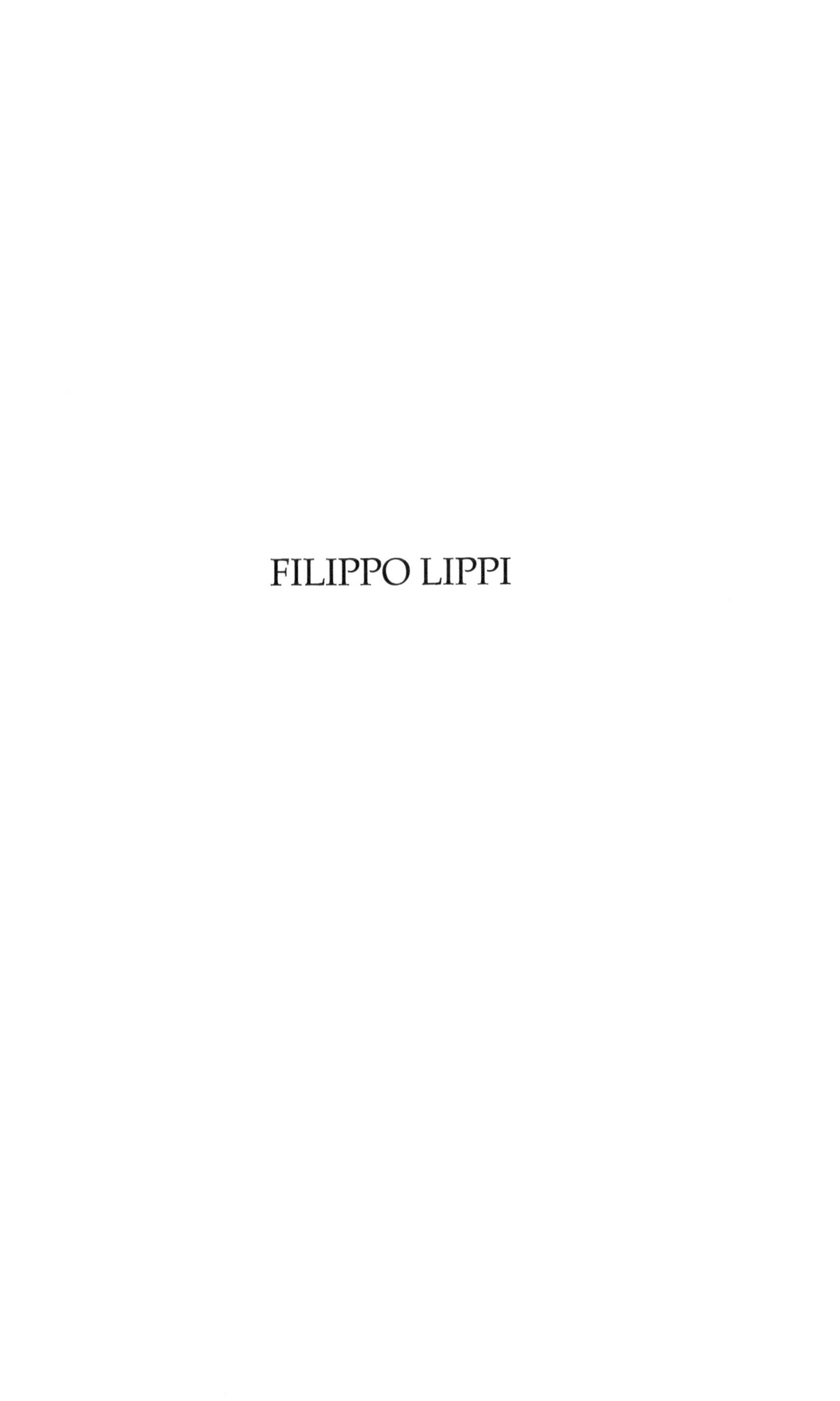

FILIPPO LIPPI

FILIPPO LIPPI

BY P. G. KONODY

CRESCENT MOON

First published 1901. This edition © 2021.

Set in Book Antiqua 10 on 14pt.
Designed by Radiance Graphics.

Thanks to the authors and publishers quoted.

British Library Cataloguing in Publication data

ISBN-13 9781861716514

CRESCENT MOON PUBLISHING
P.O. Box 1312, Maidstone, Kent, ME14 5XU
Great Britain, www.crmoon.com

CONTENTS

NOTE ON THE TEXT

The text is from *Filippo Lippi* by Paul Konody, published by Frederick A. Stokes, New York, 1901.

The illustrations in the original text are included in the illustrations section, along with many other works.

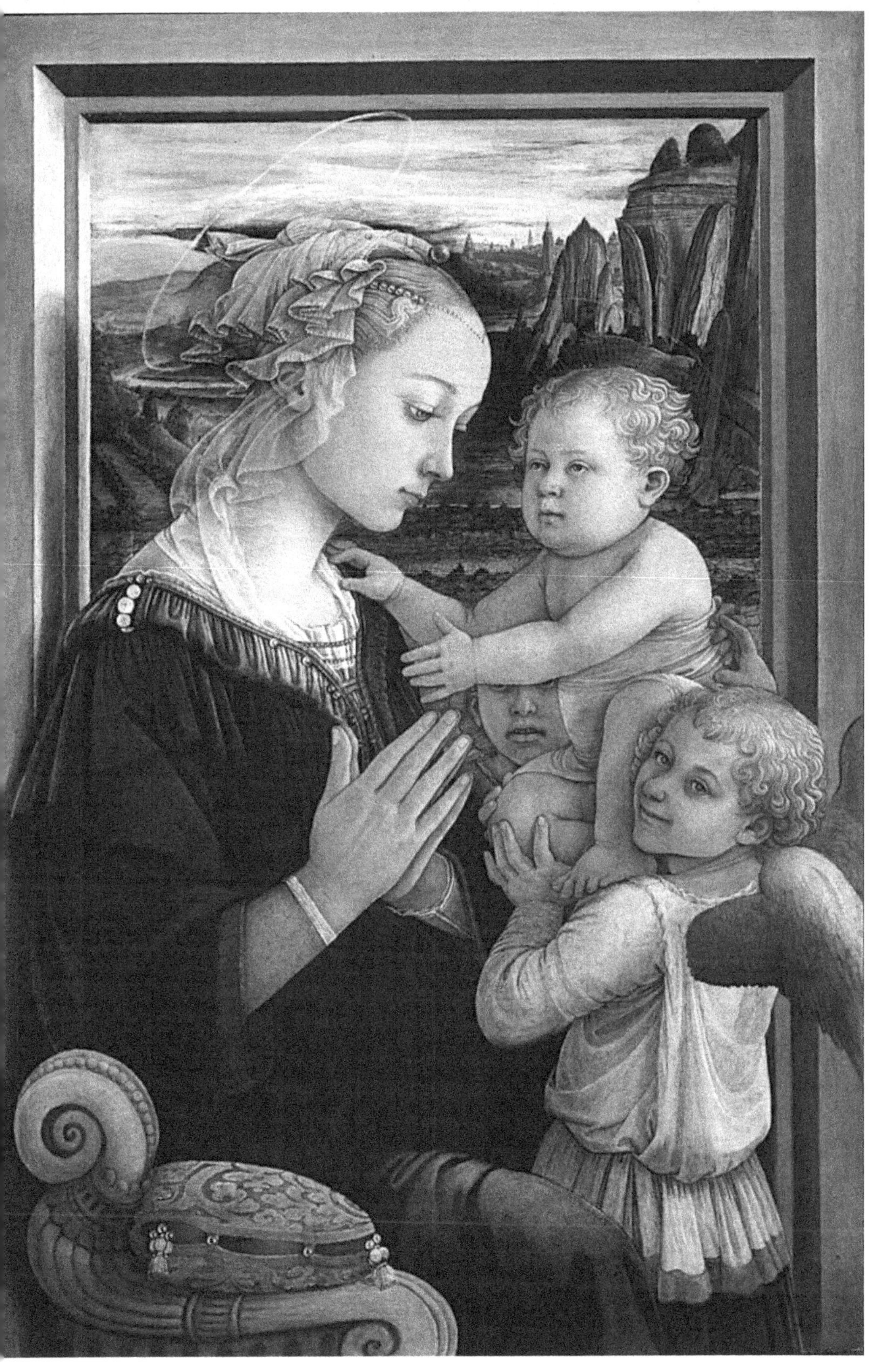

Fra Filippo Lippi, The Madonna and Child With Two Angels, Uffizi

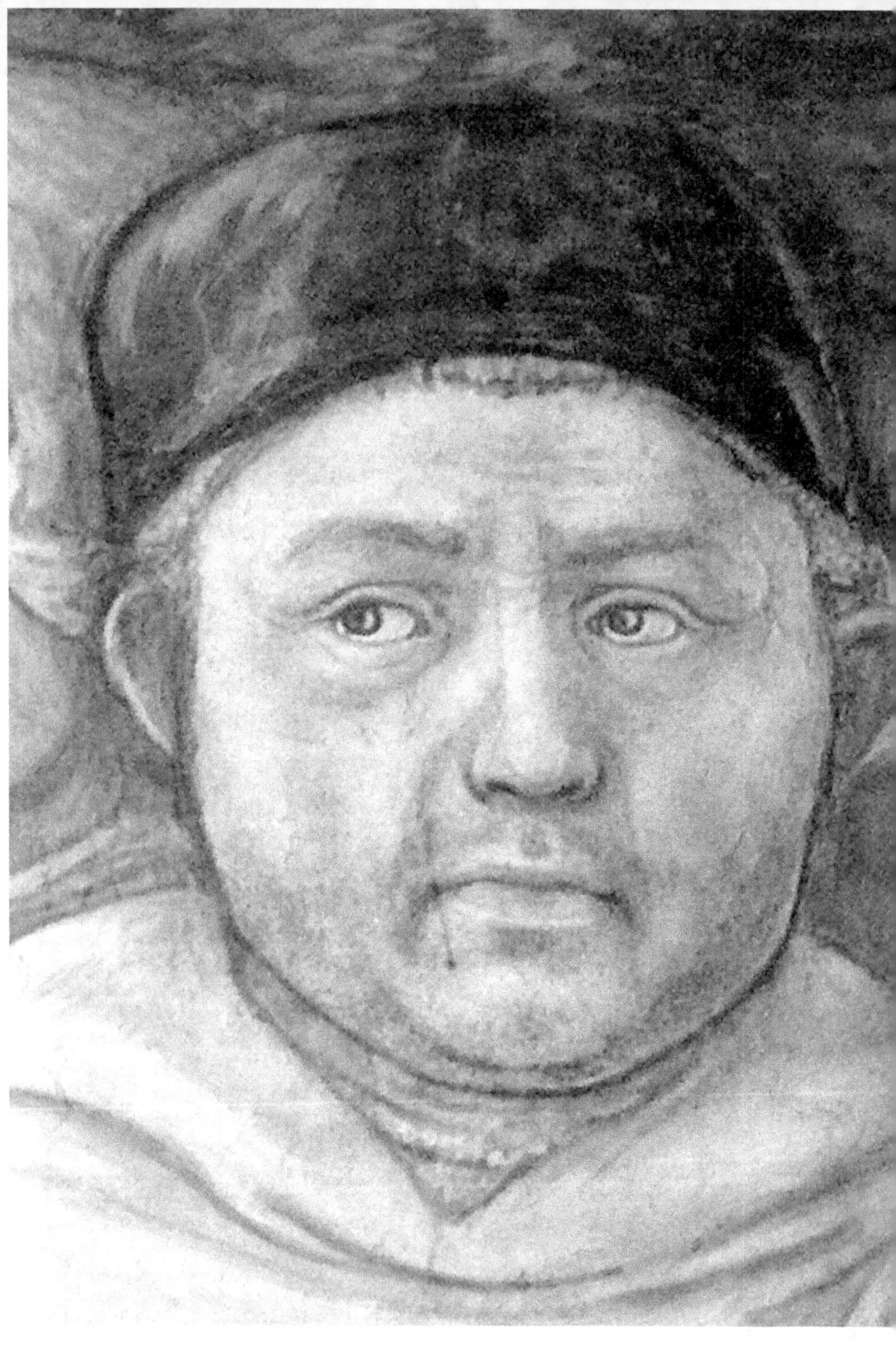

Fra Filippo Lippi, Self-Portrait

I

IN Vasari's gossipy *Lives of the Painters*, and indeed in most art histories written before the era of scientific critical research, there is an inclination, in the absence of documentary material, to reconstruct the old masters' characters and lives from the evidence of their extant works. Many a charming legend, that was originally suggested by the expression of the painter's personality in his art, and has been handed down from generation to generation, had to be shelved as dusty archives yielded new knowledge of indisputable prosaic facts to the diligent searcher. Whilst the serious student owes a debt of deep gratitude to those who devote their time and labour to the investigation of documentary evidence, and to establishing critical standards for the sifting of the great masters' works from those of their followers and imitators, the elimination of romance from the history of art is a hindrance rather than a help to the ordinary person who cares not a jot about morphological characteristics, but loves nevertheless to spend an hour now and then in communion with the old masters. For him, paradoxical though it may seem, there is more significant truth in many an entirely fictitious anecdote, than in the dry facts recorded by the conscientious historian.

Thus we know now that Domenico Veneziano outlived Andrea dal Castagno by several years, and could therefore not have been foully murdered by his jealous rival. But does not the fable of this act of violence, suggested no doubt by the fierceness and rugged strength of Andrea's art, help the layman to understand and appreciate the qualities which constitute the greatness of that art? We know now that Fra Angelico, far from accounting it a sin to paint from the nude, was an eager student of human anatomy; but the stories told of his piety and angelic sweetness have become so fused with everybody's conception of the Dominican friar's art, that even those to whom the spiritual significance of art is a sealed book, search almost instinctively for signs of religious fervour and exaltation in Fra Angelico's paintings. The stories of Sodoma's habits of life and of his strange doings at Mont' Oliveto belong probably to the realm of fiction, but they serve to explain and accentuate the worldly tendencies of his artistic achievement.

In these instances, to which many others might easily be added, the artists' personality and manner of life have been fancifully reconstructed from the character of their work. Very different is the case of Fra Filippo Lippi. Here criticism has seized upon certain authentic facts of the Carmelite friar's life and amorous adventures – facts that in their main current have been established beyond the possibility of dispute, even though they have been embroidered upon by imaginative pens – and has dealt with his art in the light of that knowledge, reading into his paintings not only his artistic emotions, but his personal desires and passions. Only thus can it be explained that generation after generation of writers on art have misconstrued the exquisite and touching innocence and virgin purity of his Madonna type into an expression of sensuality. Again and again we read about the pronounced worldliness of Fra Filippo's religious paintings, about their lack of spiritual significance and devout feeling.

Vasari, of course, is the fountain-head of this misconception of the Carmelite's art. According to the Aretine biographer, "it was said that Fra Filippo was much addicted to the pleasures of sense, insomuch that he would give all he possessed to secure the gratification of whatever inclination might at the moment be predominant, but if he could by no means accomplish his wishes, he would then depict the object which had attracted his attention in his paintings, and endeavour by discoursing and reasoning with himself to diminish the violence of his inclination. It was known that, while occupied in the pursuit of his pleasures, the works undertaken by him received little or none of his attention."

It so happens that many of the discreditable incidents of the friar's life, recorded by Vasari, have been confirmed by documentary evidence. There is not a shadow of doubt that Fra Filippo did abduct the nun Lucrezia Buti from her convent; that Filippino Lippi was the offspring of this illicit union; and that the Frate subsequently did not avail himself of the special papal dispensation to wed the nun. There is also abundant proof to show that Fra Filippo, in spite of the high esteem in which he was held as an artist, and which caused him to be entrusted with many a remunerative commission, was for ever in financial straits, was involved in many vexatious law cases, attempted to cheat his own assistants, and had no hesitation to break faith with his patrons. But all this does not affect his art. To read sensuality into his types of womanhood can only be the result of prejudice, of approaching his pictures in the light of the knowledge gathered from the pages of the chroniclers. Worldly he is compared with the pure, exalted spirituality of the Dominican Fra Angelico, but only in so far as he belonged already to the new era which had discovered, and revelled in, the visible beauty of this world of ours, whilst Fra Angelico, his contemporary, still belongs to the earlier age that looked to the empyrean for all true happiness. The art of both masters is planted in Gothic soil, though it bore different fruit, that of Fra Angelico being still essentially Gothic, though often tinged with a Renaissance flavour, whilst that of Fra Filippo has all the richness and fullness of the Renaissance, of which he was one of the great initiators.

That such conceptions as the Virgin in National Gallery "Annunciation," or the lovely Madonna in the *tondo* at the Palazzo Pitti, and many other authentic works by the master, are lacking in spirituality of expression, cannot be seriously maintained by anybody who approaches these pictures with an open mind and judges the artist by his achievement, not by his manner of life. Even Mr. Berenson, the most authoritative modern critic of Italian art, denies Fra Filippo a "profound sense of either material or spiritual significance - the essential qualifications of the real artist," although he admits in the same essay[1] that "his real place is with the genre painters, only his genre *was that of the soul,* as that of others - of Benozzo Gozzoli, for example - was of the body." Browning, with the true poet's intuition, states the case of Fra Filippo more clearly than the vast majority of professional critics from Vasari to the present day, when he makes the friar exclaim:

"... Now is this sense, I ask?
A fine way to paint soul, by painting body
So ill, the eye can't stop there, must go further
And can't fare worse!...

.....

Why can't a painter lift each foot in turn,
Left foot and right foot, go a double step,
Make his flesh liker and his soul more like,
Both in their order?...

.....

Suppose I've made her eyes all right and blue,
Can't I take breath and try to add life's flash,
And then add soul and heighten them threefold?"

1 *The Florentine Painters of the Renaissance,* by Bernhard Berenson (G. P. Putnam's Sons).

II

Whereas all questions concerning Fra Filippo's artistic education remain largely a matter of conjecture and deduction, there is no lack of documentary material for a fairly accurate reconstruction of his life. Vasari remains, of course, the basis for any such attempt; but the archives of Florence and Prato have yielded a rich harvest of contemporary records, on the strength of which it is possible to clear up the contradictions and to correct the numerous errors that have crept into Vasari's life of *The Florentine Painter, Fra Filippo Lippi*.

Filippo was the son of Tommaso di Lippo, a butcher in a poor quarter of Florence, and of Mona Antonia di Bindo Sernigi. None of the various dates given in his wonted loose fashion by Vasari for the birth of the artist, accords with ascertainable facts, which point to the years 1406 to 1409, with probability favouring the earlier date. According to a document in the Archivio di Stato in Florence, confirmed by an entry in the account books of the convent of the Carmine, in which "Philippus Tomasi" is stated to have received his garments at the expense of that establishment, Filippo took the habit in the year 1421. There are no reasons to doubt Milanesi's well-reasoned suggestion that the artist was fifteen years of age when he took the vow – which would place the year of his birth about 1406.

"By the death of his father," continues Vasari, "he was left a friendless orphan at the age of two years, his mother having also died shortly after his birth. The child was for some time under the care of a certain Mona Lapaccia, his aunt, the sister of his father, who brought him up with great difficulty till he had attained his eighth year, when, being no longer able to support the burden of his maintenance, she placed him in the convent of the Carmelites." Since, however, an income-tax return, discovered by Milanesi, proves Mona Antonia, Filippo's mother, to have been still alive in 1427, and apparently in tolerably comfortable circumstances, this account of Filippo's sad childhood must be relegated to the sphere of fiction. Destined for the Church, he was presumably at the age of eight placed with the Carmelites to be prepared for his vocation. That he showed no inclination for book-learning and "manifested the utmost dullness and incapacity in letters," and that he preferred to daub his and the other boys' books with caricatures, need not be doubted, for his extant letters prove him to have been strikingly illiterate even for his days. Nor is Filippo the only artist who evinced an early inclination for the artistic profession in this manner.

And now Vasari loses himself in a tangle of incorrect and contradictory assertions. First, that the Brancacci Chapel of the Carmine had "then" just been finished by Masaccio, and so delighted the young Carmelite that he "frequented it daily for his recreation," and so completely absorbed Masaccio's style "that many affirmed the spirit of Masaccio to have entered the body of Fra Filippo." At this period he painted several frescoes in the Carmine, and one in *terra verde* in the cloister of that church. As a result of the high praise bestowed upon him for these early efforts, "he formed his resolution at the age of seventeen, and boldly threw off the clerical habit."

To begin with, the account books of the Carmine show that Fra Filippo remained at that monastic establishment at least until 1431, when he was about twenty-five years of age. That even then he did not throw off his clerical habit is clearly proved by the fact that he subsequently held the posts of abbot of S. Quirico a Legnaja, and of chaplain to the nuns of Sta. Margherita at Prato.

Of the early frescoes recorded by Vasari and other writers, every vestige has disappeared, so that it is impossible to trace through them the supposed direct or indirect teaching of Masaccio. But there is something wrong about the dates. Masaccio wrought his Carmine frescoes between 1425 and 1427, so that his could not possibly have been the earliest influence upon the young monk's impressionable mind. Nor is there even a hint of Masaccio's monumental style in the earliest known works by Filippo: the two "Nativities" in the Florence Academy, and the "Annunciation" in the Pinakothek in Munich. That Fra Filippo, like all the masters of the Florentine Renaissance, was, in his later life, powerfully influenced by the genius of Masaccio, is only natural, and cannot be doubted by anybody who has seen his frescoes at Prato. For his earliest inspiration, however, one has to look for other sources; and modern criticism is pretty well agreed upon this point, that the pictures painted by the friar in his youthful years are based on the trecento tradition, and that the only late Giottesque who could have been his master is the Camaldolese, Lorenzo Monaco.

Lorenzo Monaco's teaching, at any rate, is suggested by Fra Filippo's first "Nativity" at the Florence Academy, which suggests the methods of the school of miniaturists in which Lorenzo had been trained, although these tendencies are clearly tempered by the influence of Masolino, Masaccio's precursor in the decoration of the Brancacci Chapel, and also of Fra Angelico. Indeed, this "Nativity" was actually for a long time attributed to Masolino. Throughout his life, Fra Filippo, in his steady advance from Giottism to such triumphantly vital achievement as his Prato frescoes, evinced the greatest eagerness to absorb what was newest and best. No doubt he watched Masolino at work at the Carmine, and later on Masaccio, whose influence clearly appears in Fra Filippo's mature work. But he also learnt from the example of all the other masters who wrought in and near Florence in the early part of the fifteenth century. Sir Frederick Cook's *tondo* clearly shows the influence of Gentile da Fabriano. Of Fra Angelico we are reminded by the profound devotional feeling and mystic intentness of his early works. From Pier dei Franceschi he acquired afterwards the feeling for atmospheric effects which was unknown to the Giottesques, to Fra Angelico, and even to Masaccio. Nor did he fail to study the reliefs of Donatello, of which we are forcibly reminded by the "Madonna and Child with the laughing Angel" at the Uffizi. And since Miss Mendelssohn has shown that the dancing Salome in the Prato fresco is practically copied from the figure of "Luna descending from her Chariot" in the relief on the Endymion sarcophagus, we have proof that Lippi was also a student of the antique.

The patronage which the powerful Medici family, and especially Cosimo de' Medici, bestowed upon Fra Filippo Lippi, probably dates back to the time when the friar was still working within the walls of the Carmine. The "Nativity" (No. 79) at the Florence Academy was painted in the early thirties of the fifteenth century for Cosimo's wife, who commissioned it for the Camaldoli hermitage. For Cosimo himself he painted the two lunettes now in the National Gallery: "The Annunciation" and "St. John the Baptist with six other Saints," which were originally placed over two doors in the Riccardi Palace. Other pictures by their protégé were sent by members of the Medici family as gifts to the King of Naples and other Italian princes. And there is no lack of documentary evidence that the friar frequently petitioned members of that powerful family for pecuniary or other assistance, for his disorderly habits of life brought him into many a scrape, and resulted in constant financial stress. Thus in a letter of August 13, 1439, to Piero de' Medici, he describes himself as "one of the poorest friars in Florence," whom God left to look after six unmarried, infirm, and useless nieces. The object of the letter was to beg his patron to be supplied with wine and corn on credit.

When Cosimo was banished from Florence in 1433, and took up his residence at Padua, he was accompanied by a small army of courtiers and artists. It is very probable that Fra Filippo was of their number. Vasari's brief reference to paintings executed by the master in Padua is supported by Filarete and the Anonimo

Morelliano, and may therefore be relied upon, although every trace of these works has vanished. There is nothing in the extant records of the artist's movements to make his presence at Padua in 1433-4 appear impossible. On the other hand, Vasari's story of Filippo's capture by pirates on the coast of the Marches of Ancona, his long-extended captivity and final liberation by his master whose favour he had gained by the excellence of art, and his visit to Naples on the home journey, belongs to the realm of fable.

In or before 1437, Fra Filippo was certainly back in Florence, since the *Deliberazioni* of the Company of Orsanmichele show that in that year he was commissioned to paint the great altarpiece of the "Madonna and Child, with Angels and two Abbots" for the Barbadori Chapel in Santo Spirito, which is now one of the treasures of the Louvre. It is this picture to which Domenico Veneziano refers in a letter to Piero de' Medici, dated Perugia, April 1, 1438, asking to be entrusted with the commission for an altarpiece, since "Fra Filippo and Fra Giovanni have much work to do, and especially Fra Filippo has a panel for Santo Spirito which, should he work day and night, will not be done in five years, so great is the work." Yet in the following year we find him writing a begging letter to the same Piero de' Medici.

There can be no doubt that the gay friar led the life of a true "Bohemian" - that he was fond of women and wine, and wasted his substance in the company of his boon companions. He spent his money as rapidly as he earned it, and was therefore in constant financial difficulties, which involved him in no end of litigation. His most prosperous years apparently began in 1442, when, probably through Cosimo's intervention, Pope Eugene IV. made him rector of the parish church of S. Quirico a Legnaja, of which post he was deprived by papal decree as a result of an action brought against him by his assistant, Giovanni da Rovezzano. Giovanni sued him for the amount of forty florins due to him for work done, and Fra Filippo did not shrink from producing a forged receipt. To this at least he confessed on the rack "when he saw his intestines protruding from his wounds."

Whether much weight can be attached to a confession obtained by such means is another question, but there is nothing in the career of Fra Filippo to make such disgraceful conduct appear impossible.

An appeal to the Pope led to another investigation of the case. The judgment of the Curia was confirmed, the Pope referring on this occasion to Fra Filippo as a painter *qui plurima et nefanda scelera perpetravit*. Nevertheless, some years later, our artist is still mentioned as *rettore e commendatario di San Quirico a Legnaja*. From which it may be assumed that the judgment deprived him merely of his spiritual office, and left him in enjoyment of the revenue connected with the post.

The ups and downs of Filippo Lippi's career in the fifties of the fourteen-hundreds are more than a little confusing. Of commissions there was no lack. And certain emoluments must have come to him from his ecclesiastic appointments. His disgraceful conduct towards Giovanni da Rovezzano, and the notorious looseness of his morals - one need only recall the well-known anecdote of his escape through a window of the Medici Palace in search of amorous adventure - did not stand in the way of his being made chaplain to the nuns of S. Niccolò de' Fieri, in 1450,[2] and of Santa Margherita in Prato, in 1456. He bought a little house at Prato in 1452, and another in 1454. During this whole period he had so much work on hand that he was unable to fulfil his contracts, which led to further unpleasant litigations. Yet in 1454, as we learn from Neri di Lorenzo di Bicci's diaries, he found it advisable to deposit some gold-leaf with the said Neri, in order to save it from seizure by his creditors. On July 20, 1457, he writes to Giovanni de' Medici to ask for an advance payment for work in hand - the same work, presumably, over the execution of which he was so tardy that Francesco Cantamanti had to visit his studio daily to urge its completion on behalf of his patron. In his report to Giovanni de' Medici, dated August 31, 1457, Cantamanti states that on the preceding day Fra Filippo's studio was seized by his

2 He retained this post until July 1452.

landlord for arrears of rent.

Meanwhile the Carmelite's art had made prodigious progress. Filippo Lippi, the pupil of the last Giottesque, was now swimming abreast of the mighty current of the Renaissance. If his early Madonnas recall something of the spirituality and naïve faith of Fra Angelico, the altarpieces of his later Florentine period, and, above all, the superb "Coronation of the Virgin," painted for Sant' Ambrogio, and now in the Florence Academy, are inspired by the beauty of this visible world. The atmosphere is of this earth, and not of the celestial regions. His types are no longer ethereal, but realistically robust. In the "Coronation of the Virgin" he has left us a portrait of himself at the age of about forty, in the figure of the kneeling monk on the left, towards whom an angel raises a scroll with the lettering IS PERFECIT OPUS. The features are rather coarse and heavy, but scarcely express that low sensuality which his biographers have tried to read into them. The expression of his eyes in particular is intelligent, frank, and good-natured.

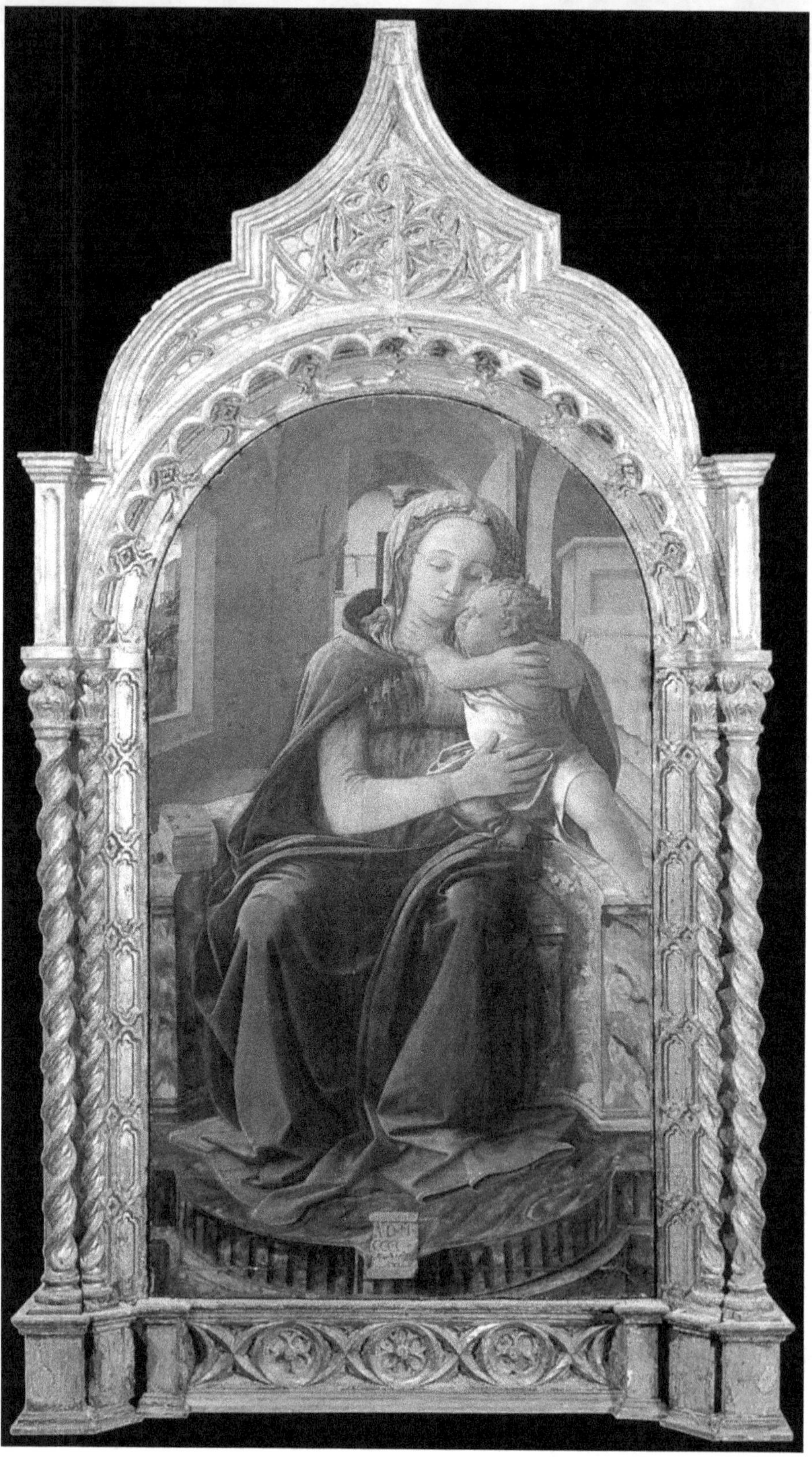

Fra Filippo Lippi, The Tarquinia Madonna, Rome

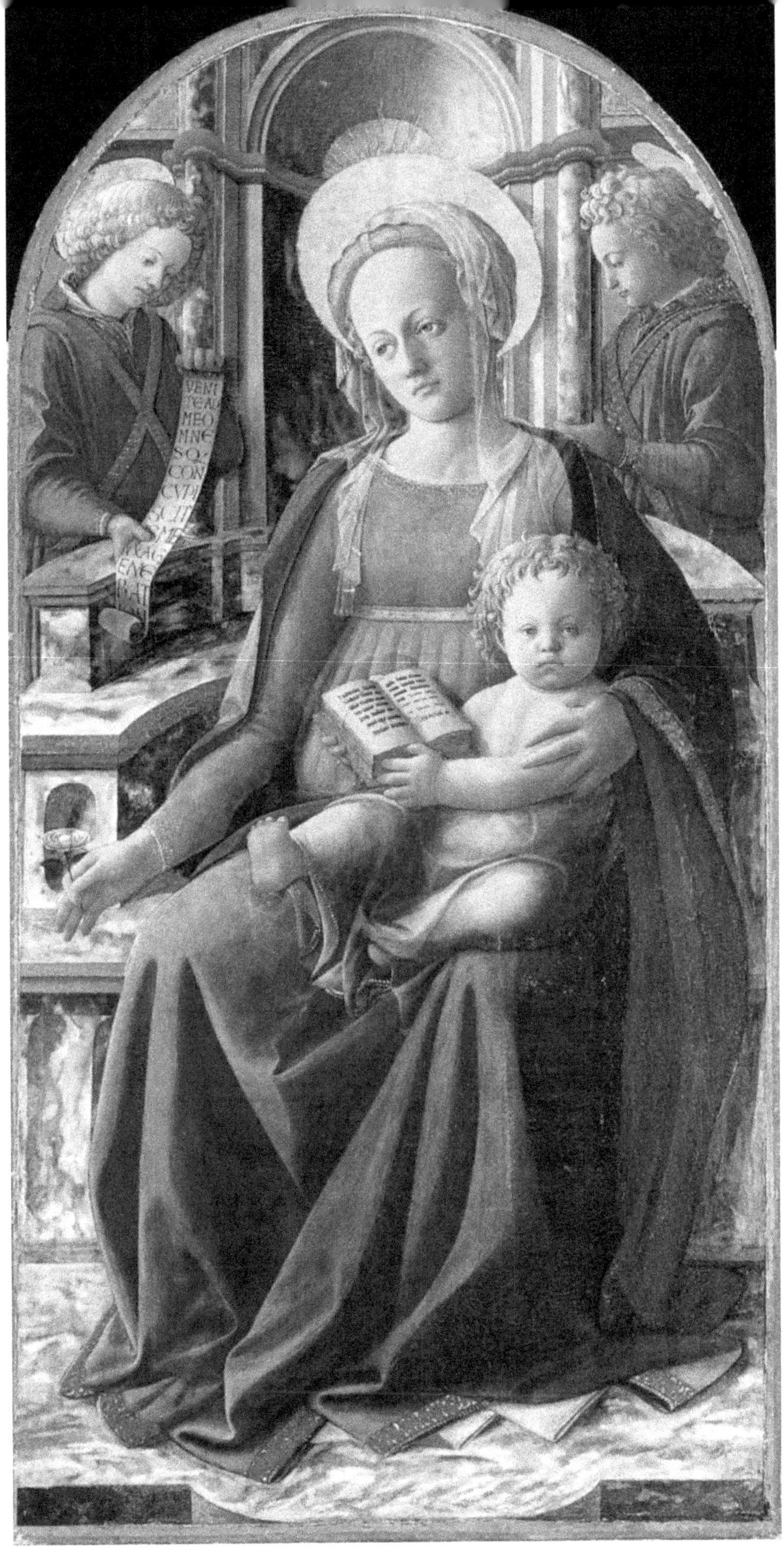

Fra Filippo Lippi, The Madonna and Child Enthroned With Two Angels, Metropolitan Museum, New York City (this page and over).

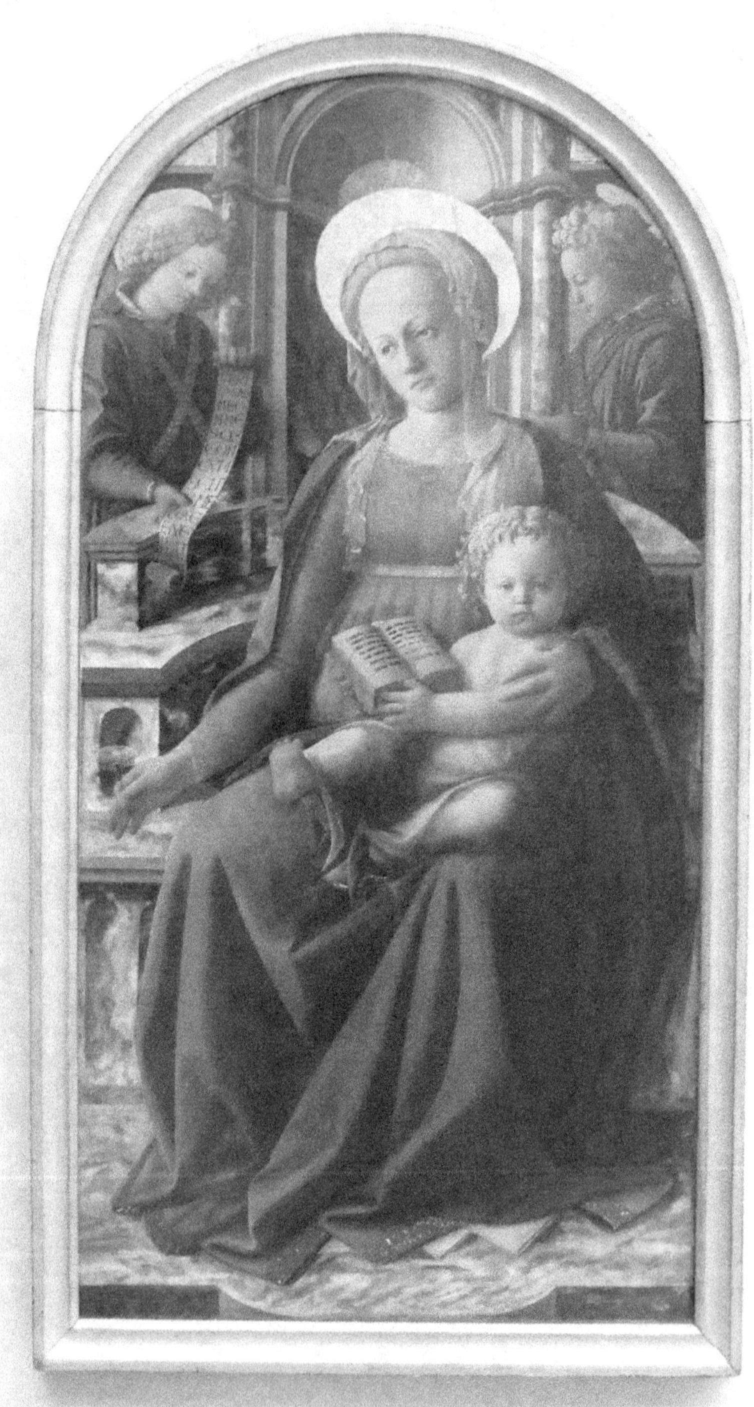

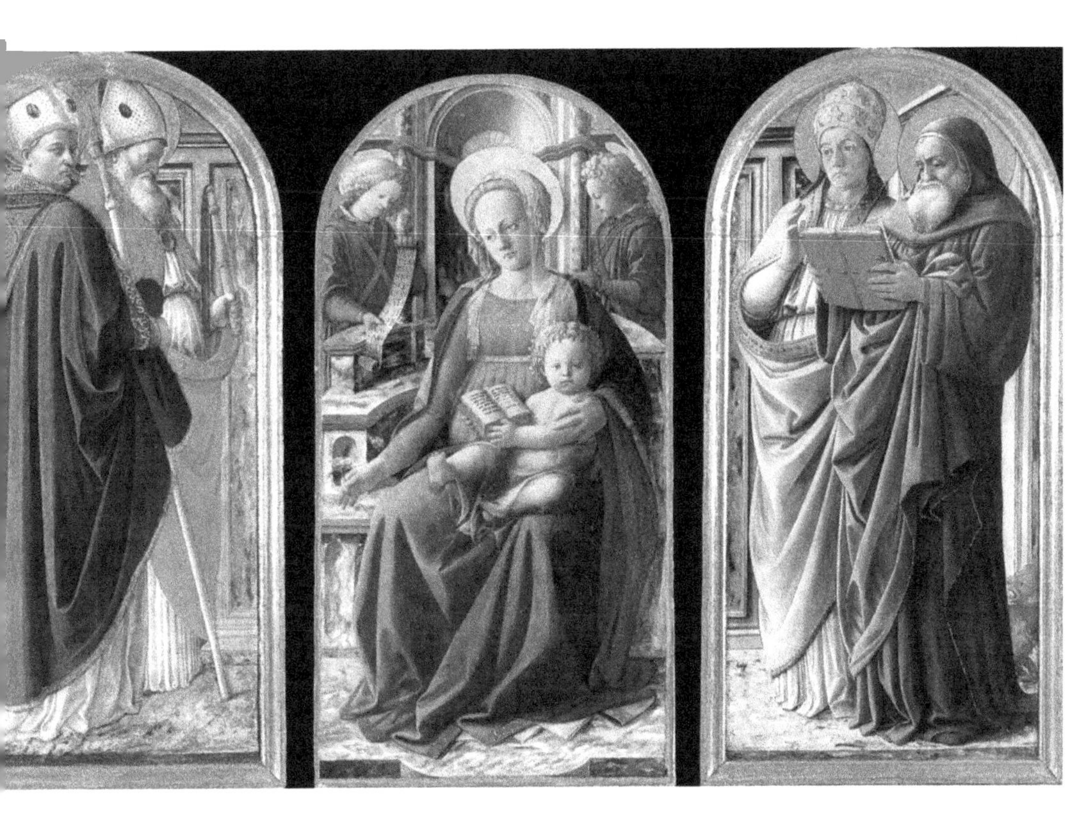

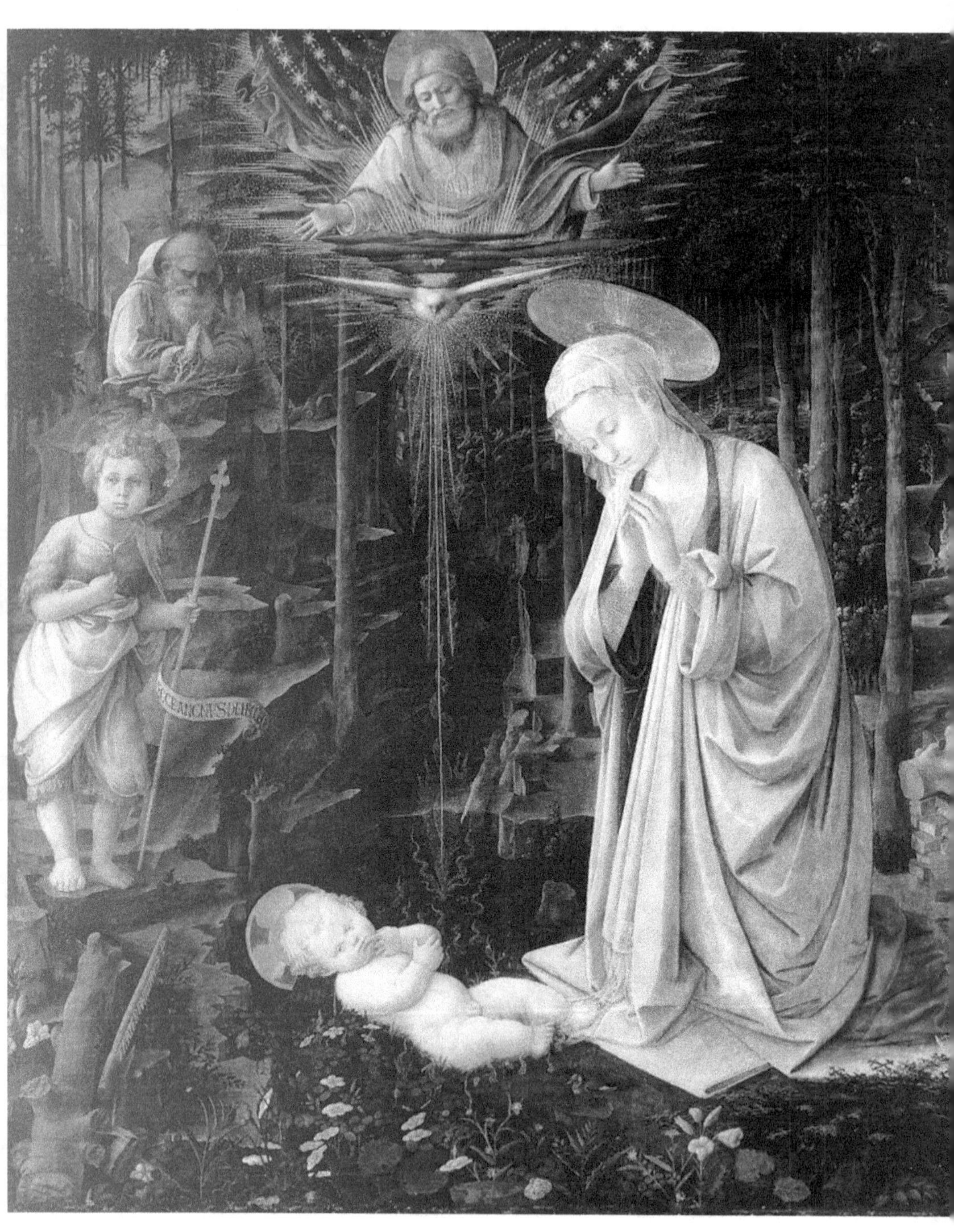

Fra Filippo Lippi, The Adoration In the Forest, Berlin

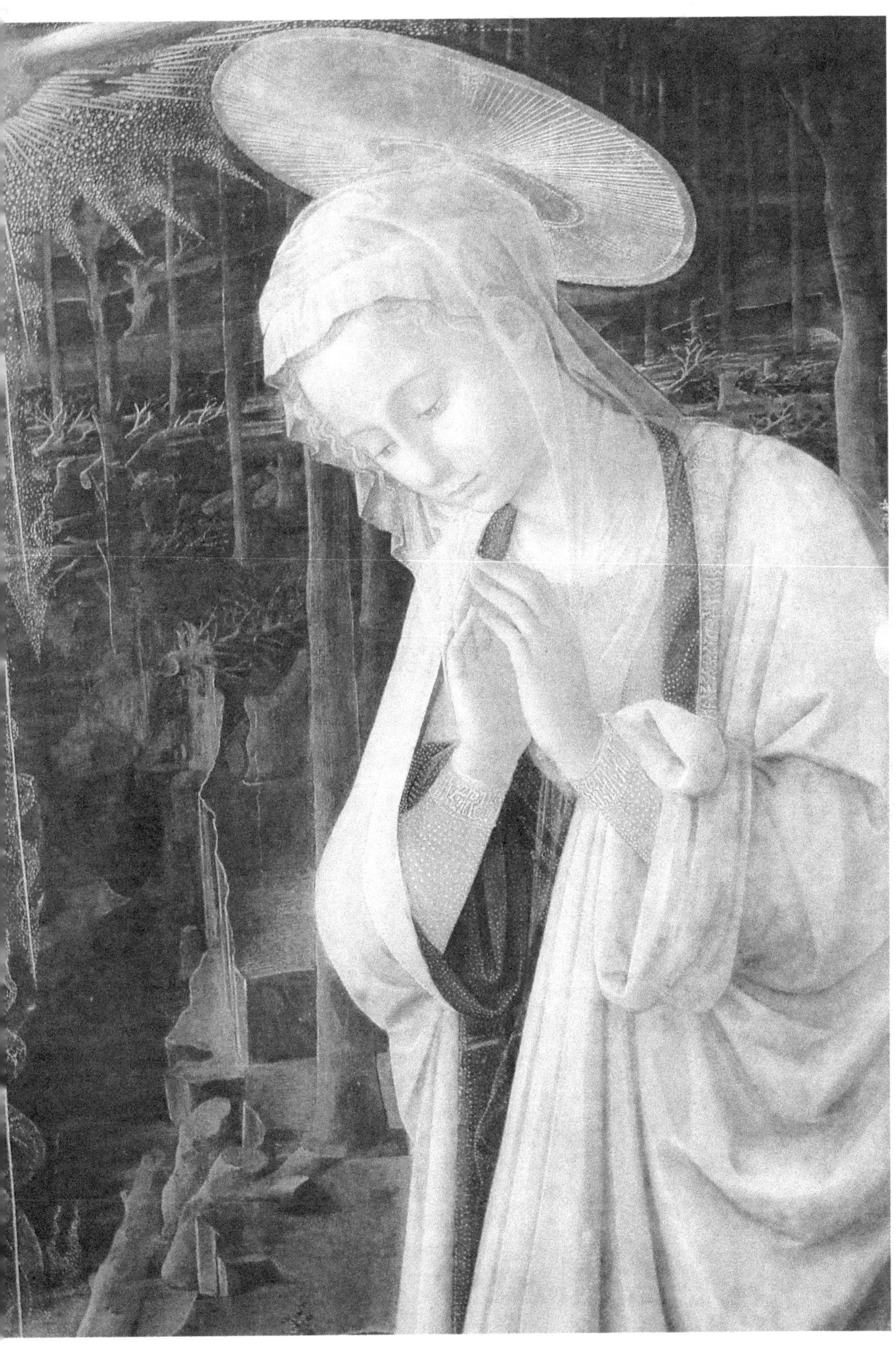

Fra Filippo Lippi, The Adoration of the Virgin, Berlin, detail

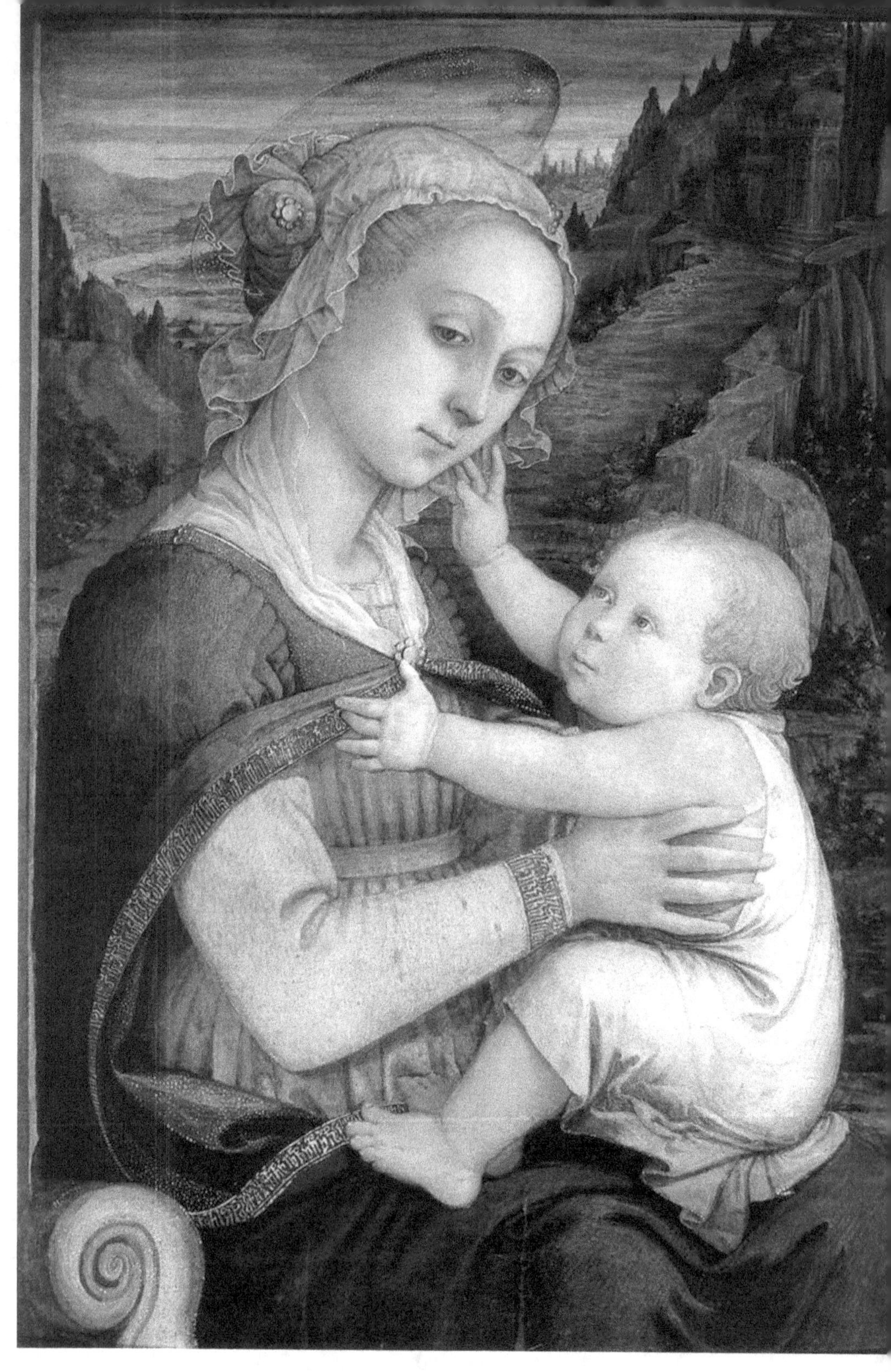

Fra Filippo Lippi, The Madonna and Child, Munich

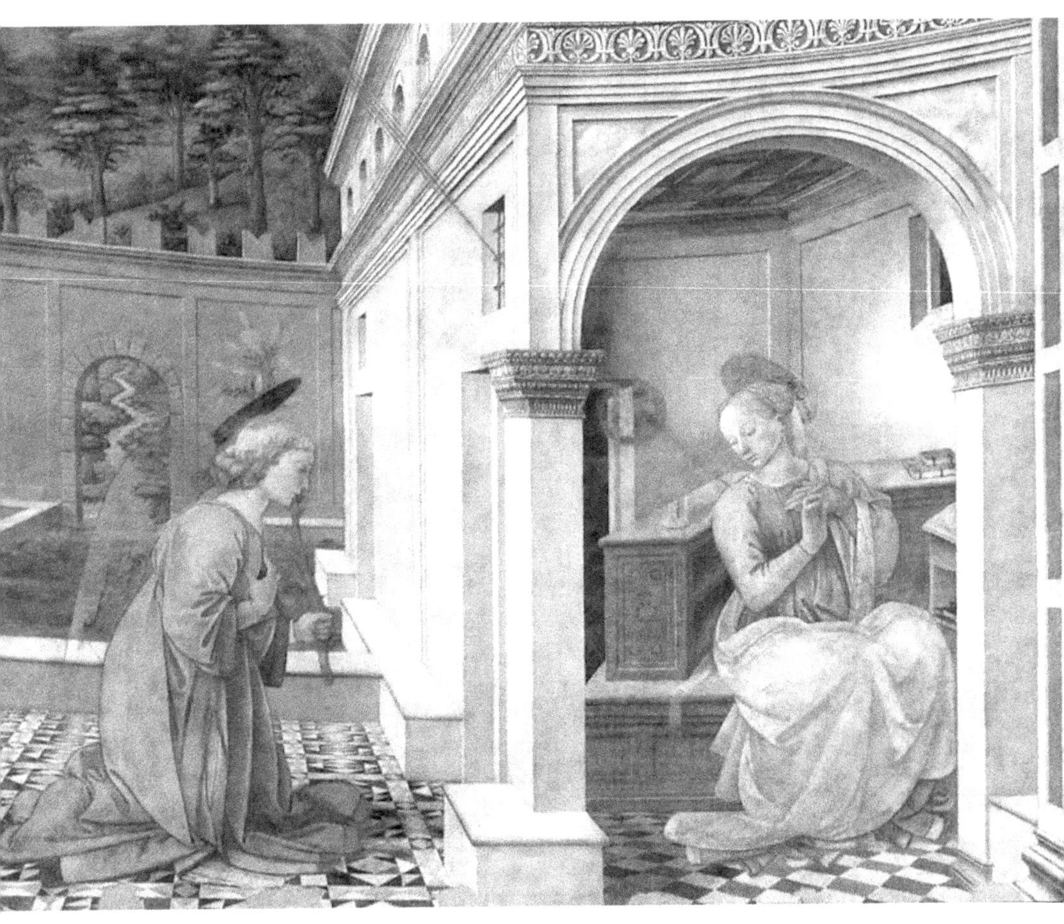

Fra Filippo Lippi, The Annunciation, 1467-69, Spoleto

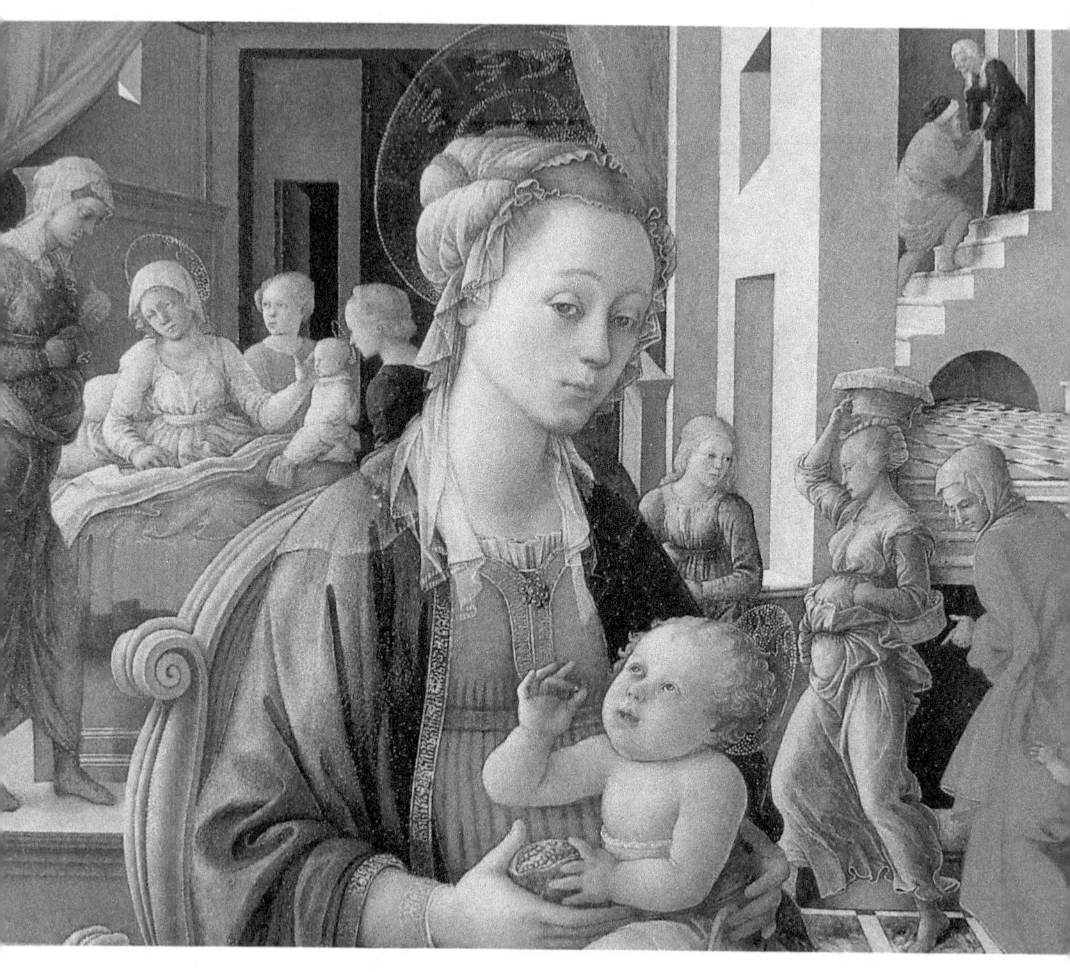

Fra Filippo Lippi, Madonna and Child With Scenes From the Life of St Anne, 1452, Pitti Palace, Florence

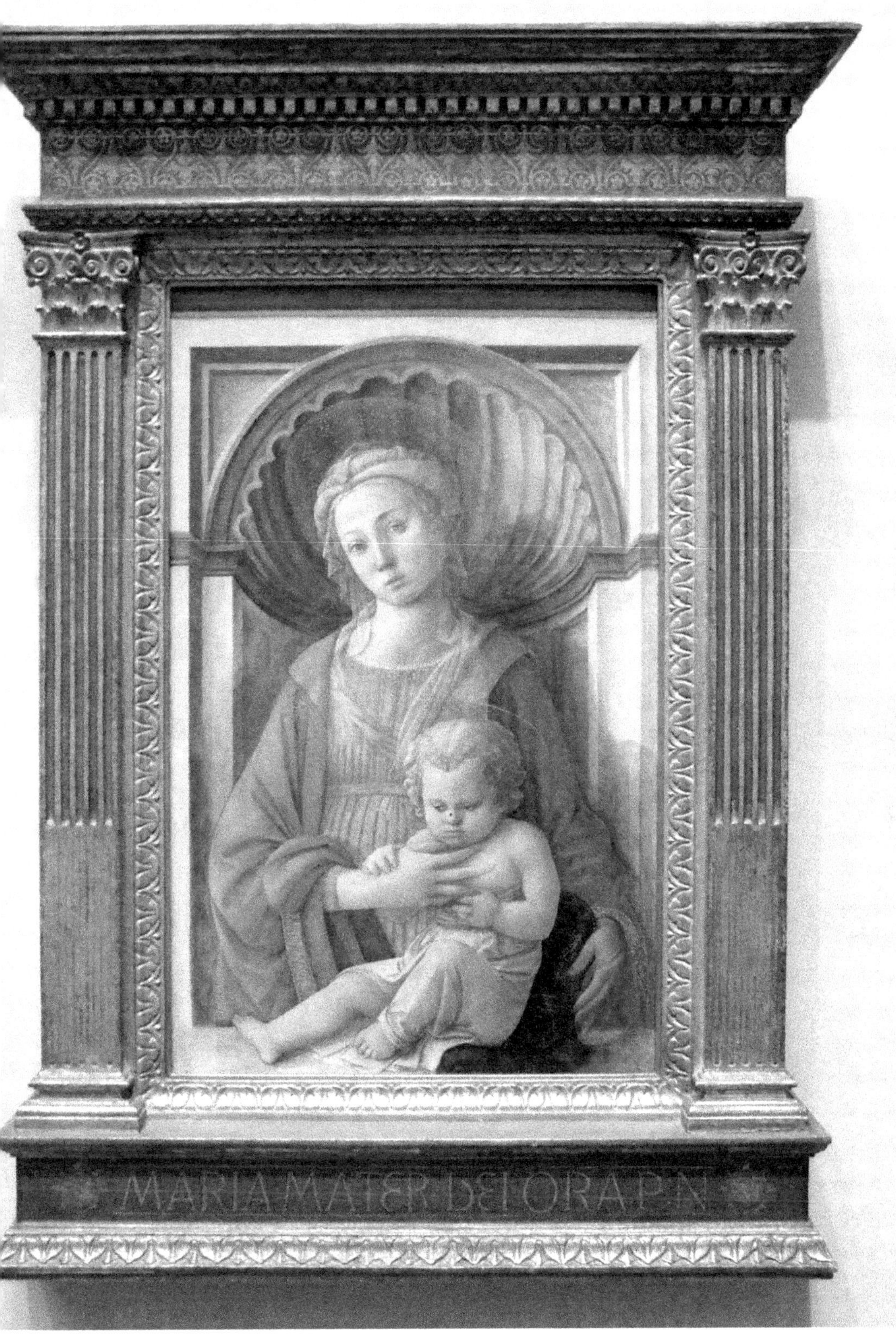

Fra Filippo Lippi, Madonna and Child, 1440-45, Washington

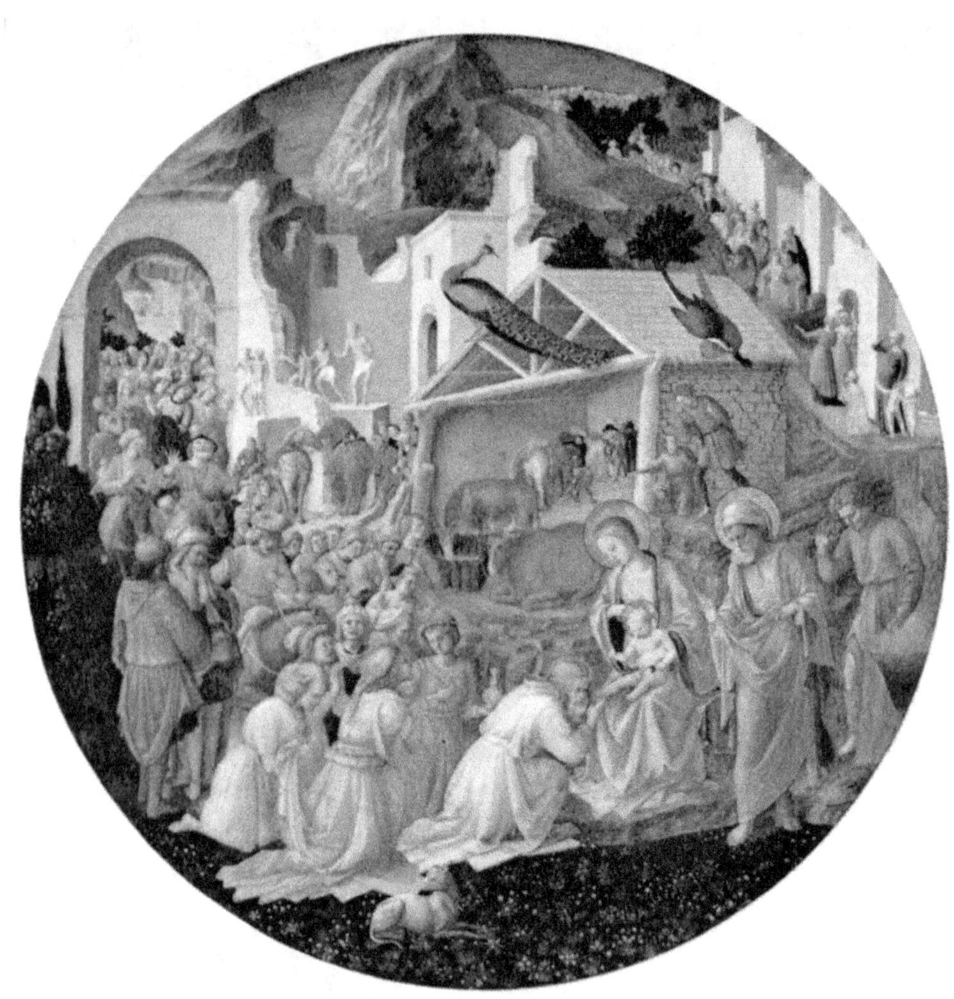

Fra Filippo Lippi with Fra Angelico, Nativity

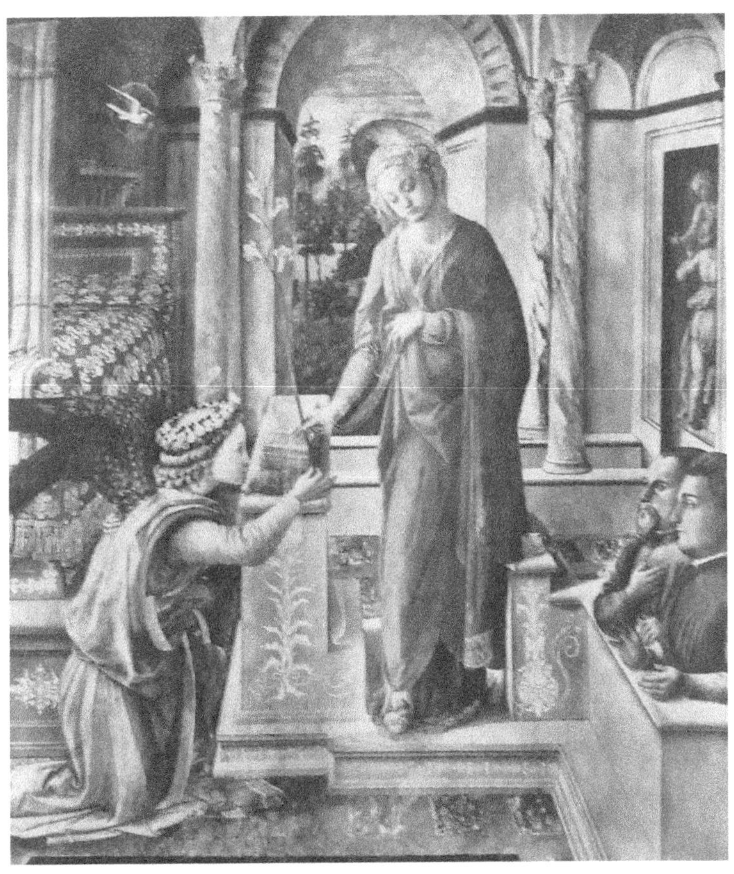

Fra Filippo Lippi, The Annunciation, 1450

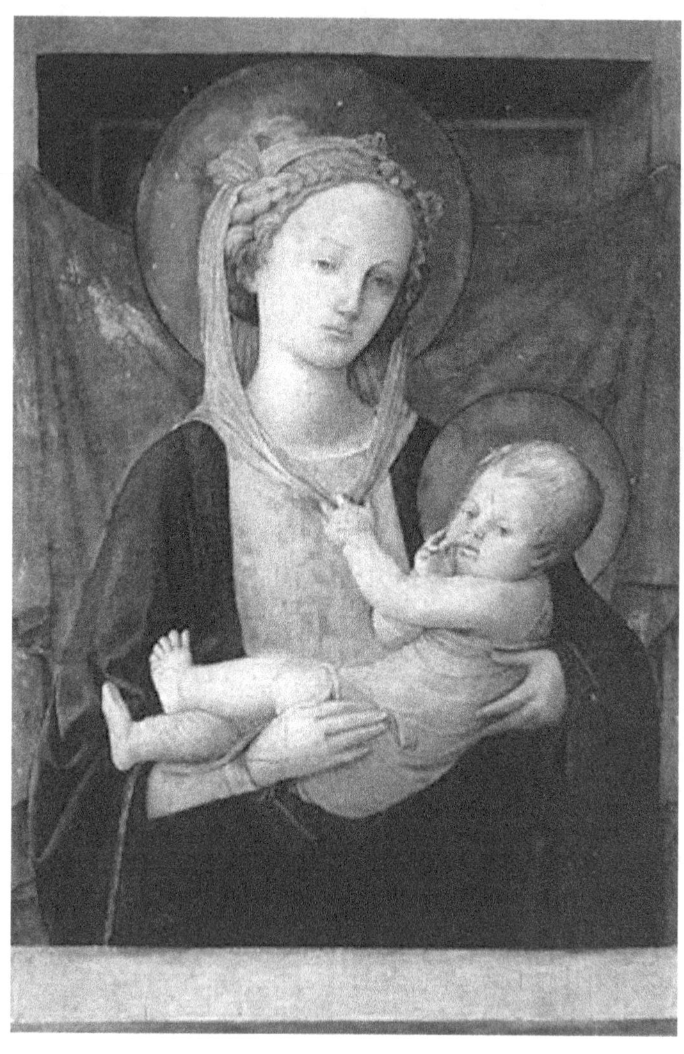

Fra Filippo Lippi, Madonna and Child, c. 1450-55,
Magnani-Rocca Foundation

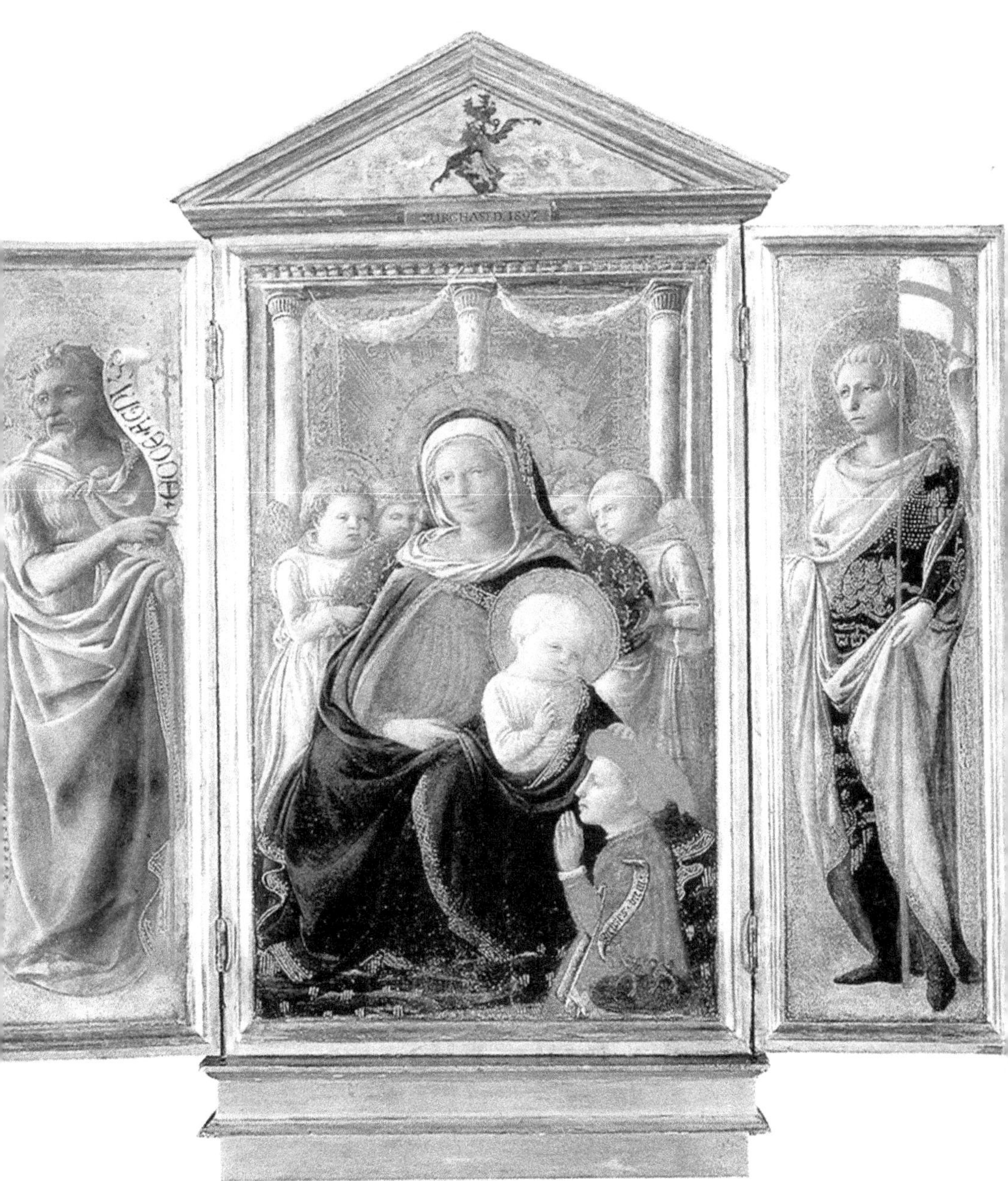

Fra Filippo Lippi, Madonna Triptych, Cambridge

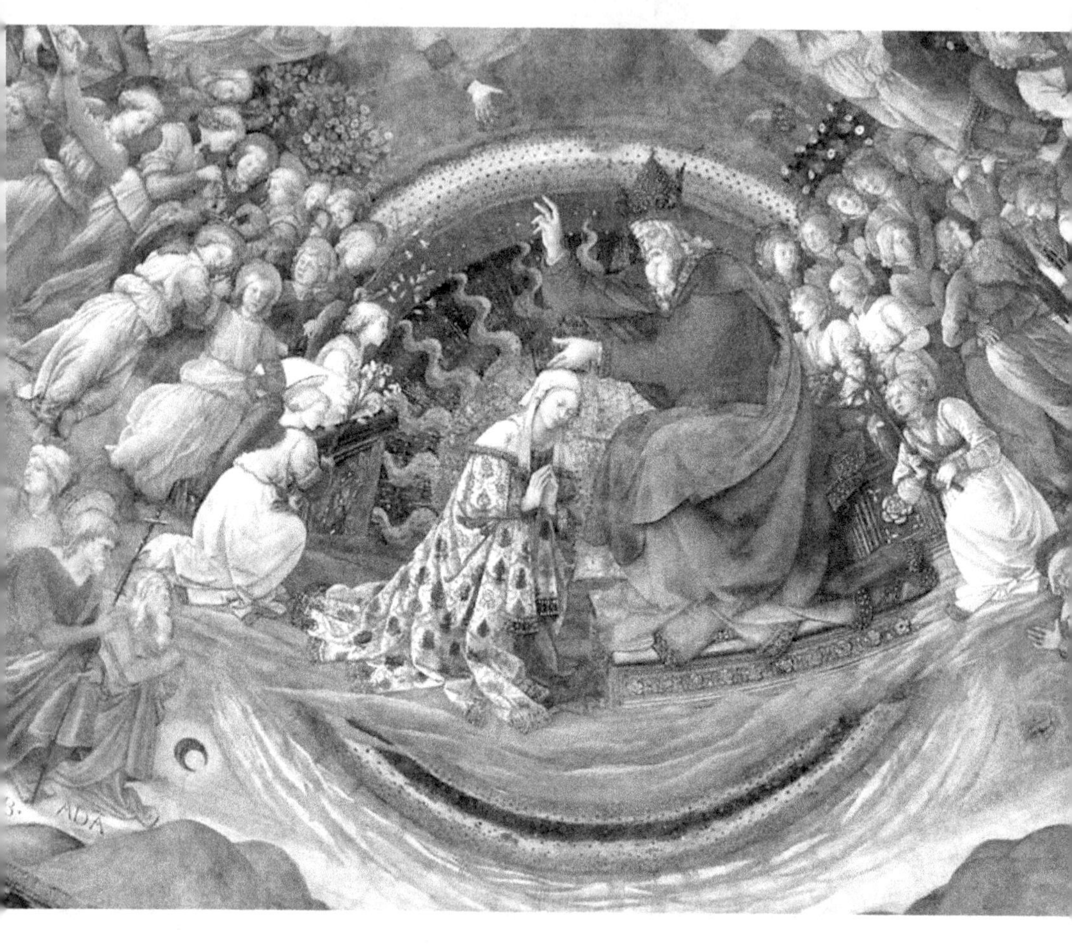

Fra Filippo Lippi, The Corononation of the Virgin

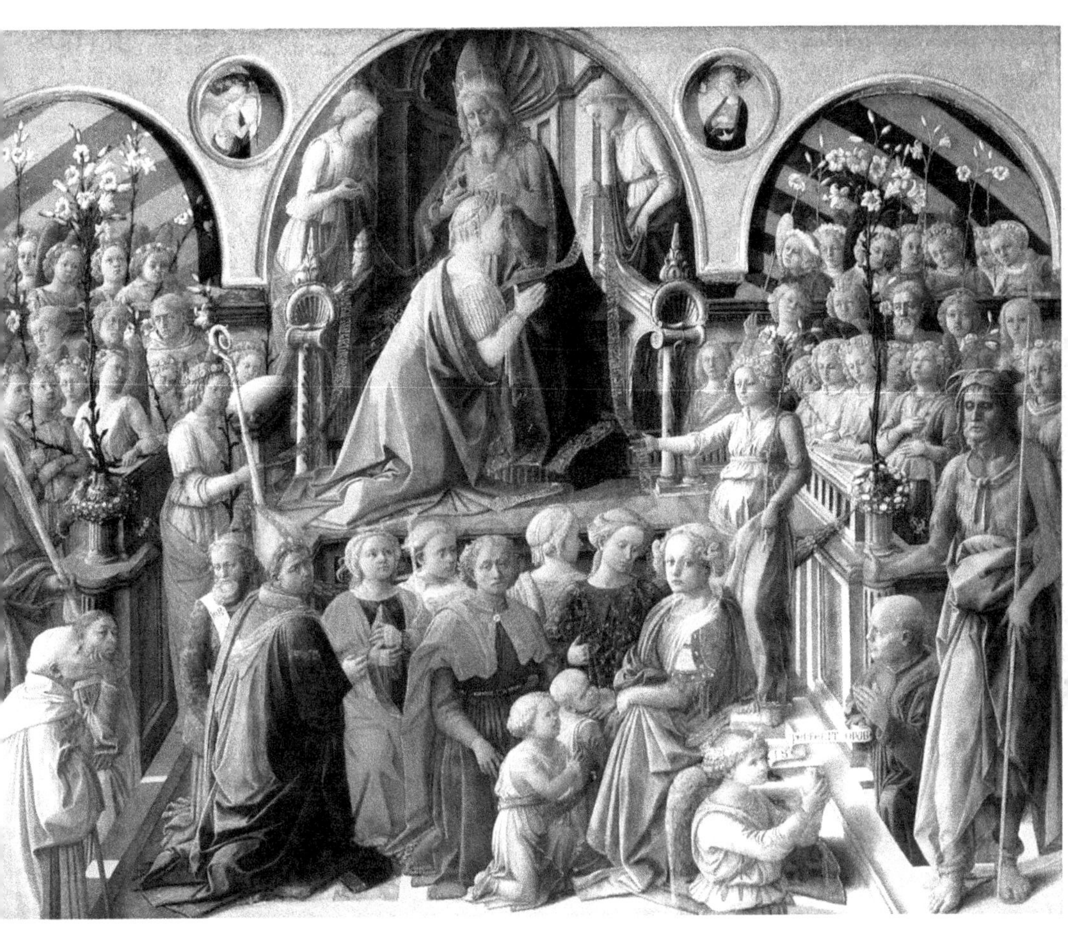

Fra Filippo Lippi, The Crowning of Mary, 1441-47, Uffizi

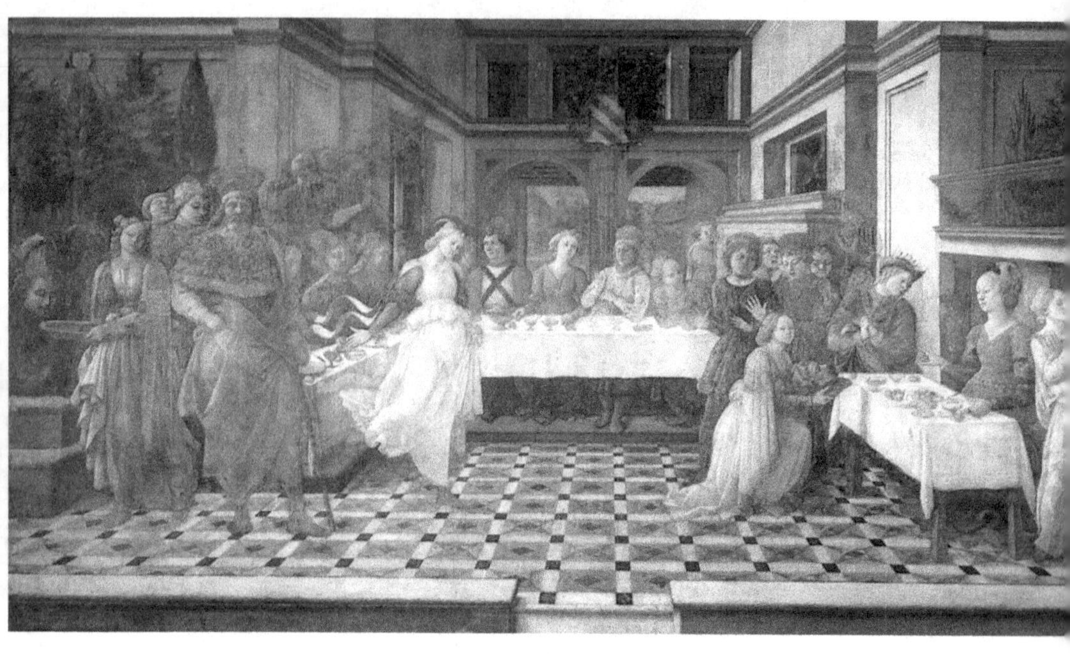

Fra Filippo Lippi, Herod's Banquet, Prato

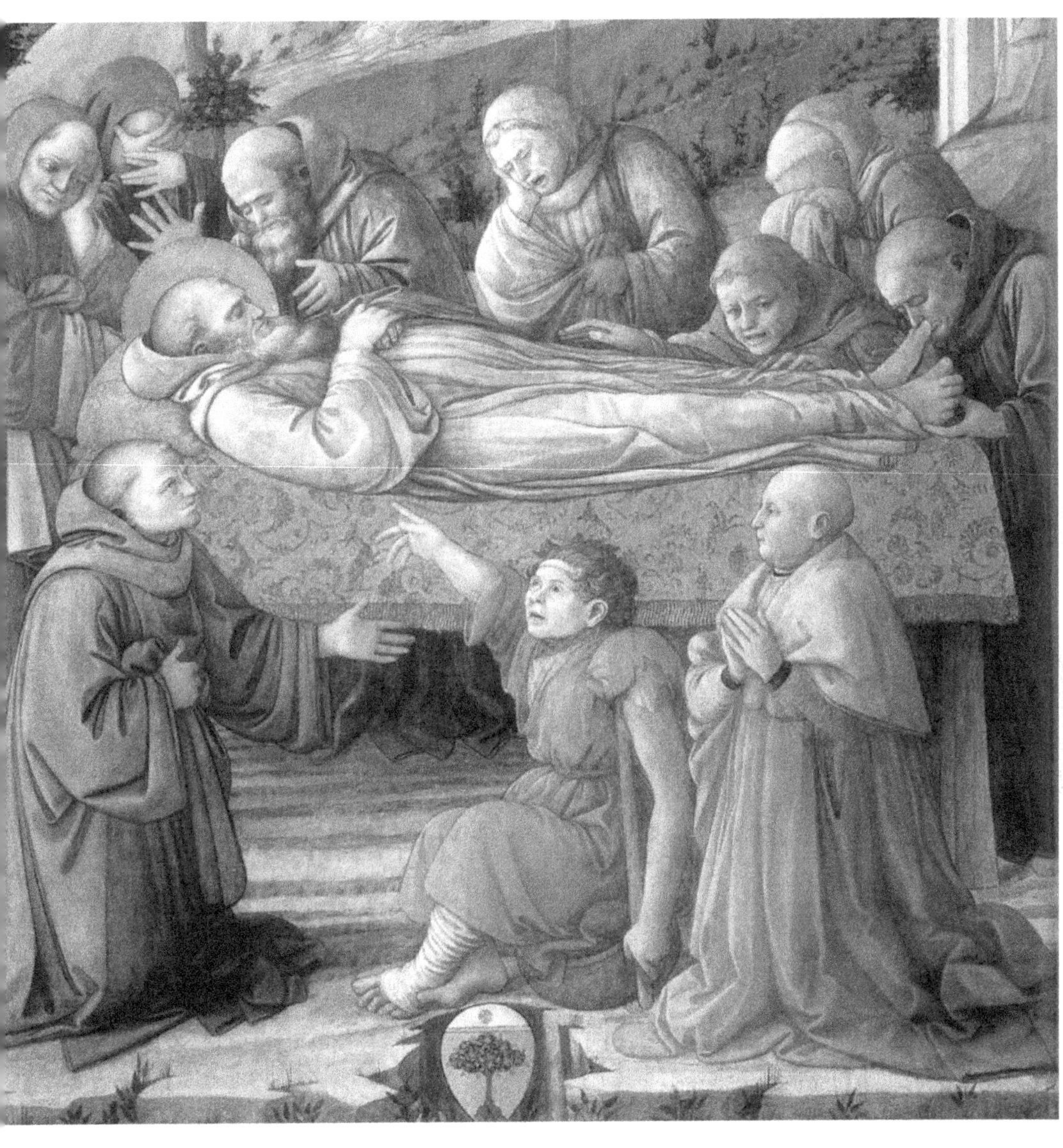

Fra Filippo Lippi, Lippi, The Funeral of St Jerome, 1452-60, Prato

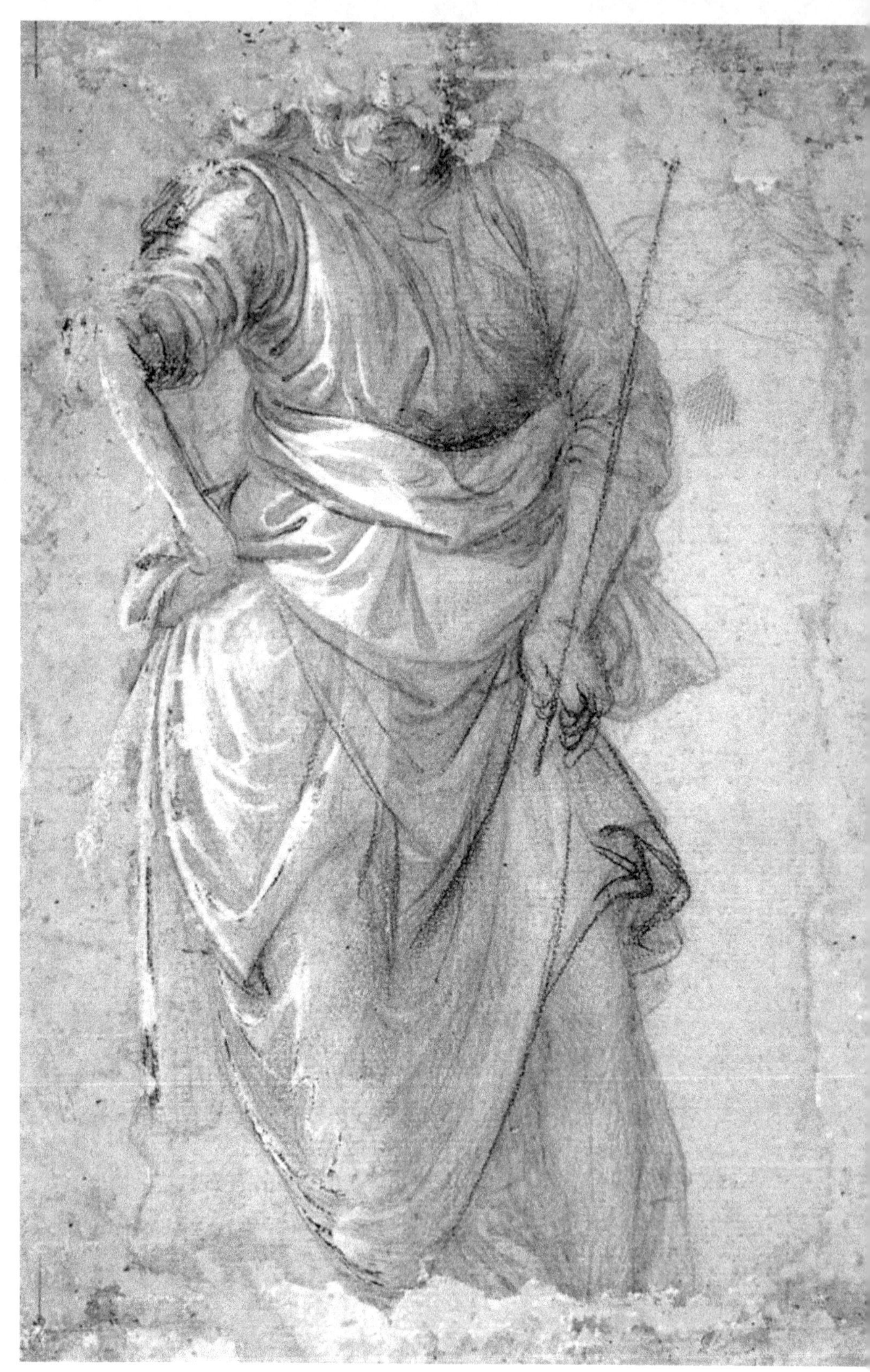

Fra Filippo Lippi, Figure Study, Uffizi Gallery

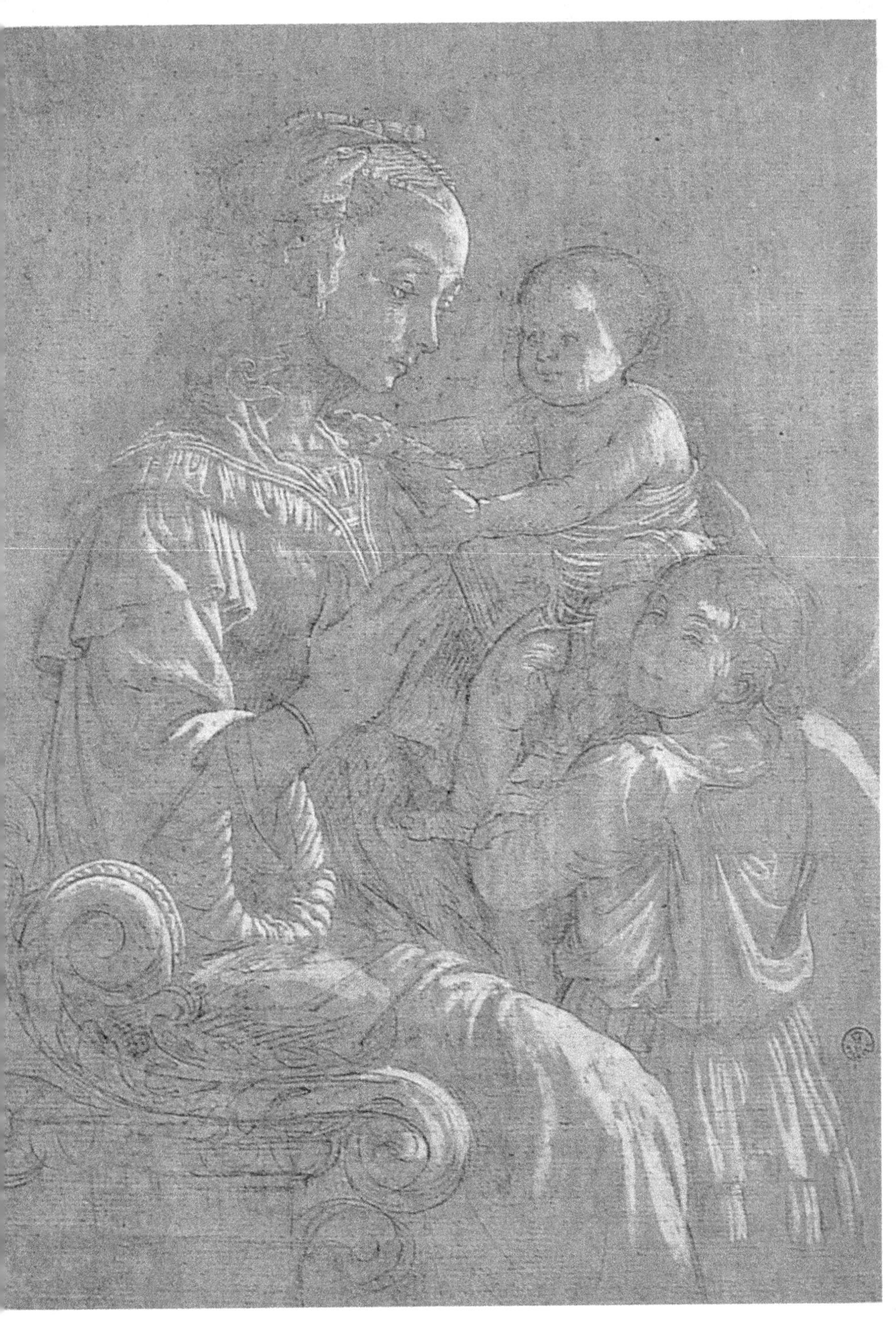

Fra Filippo Lippi, Study For Madonna and Child, 1465

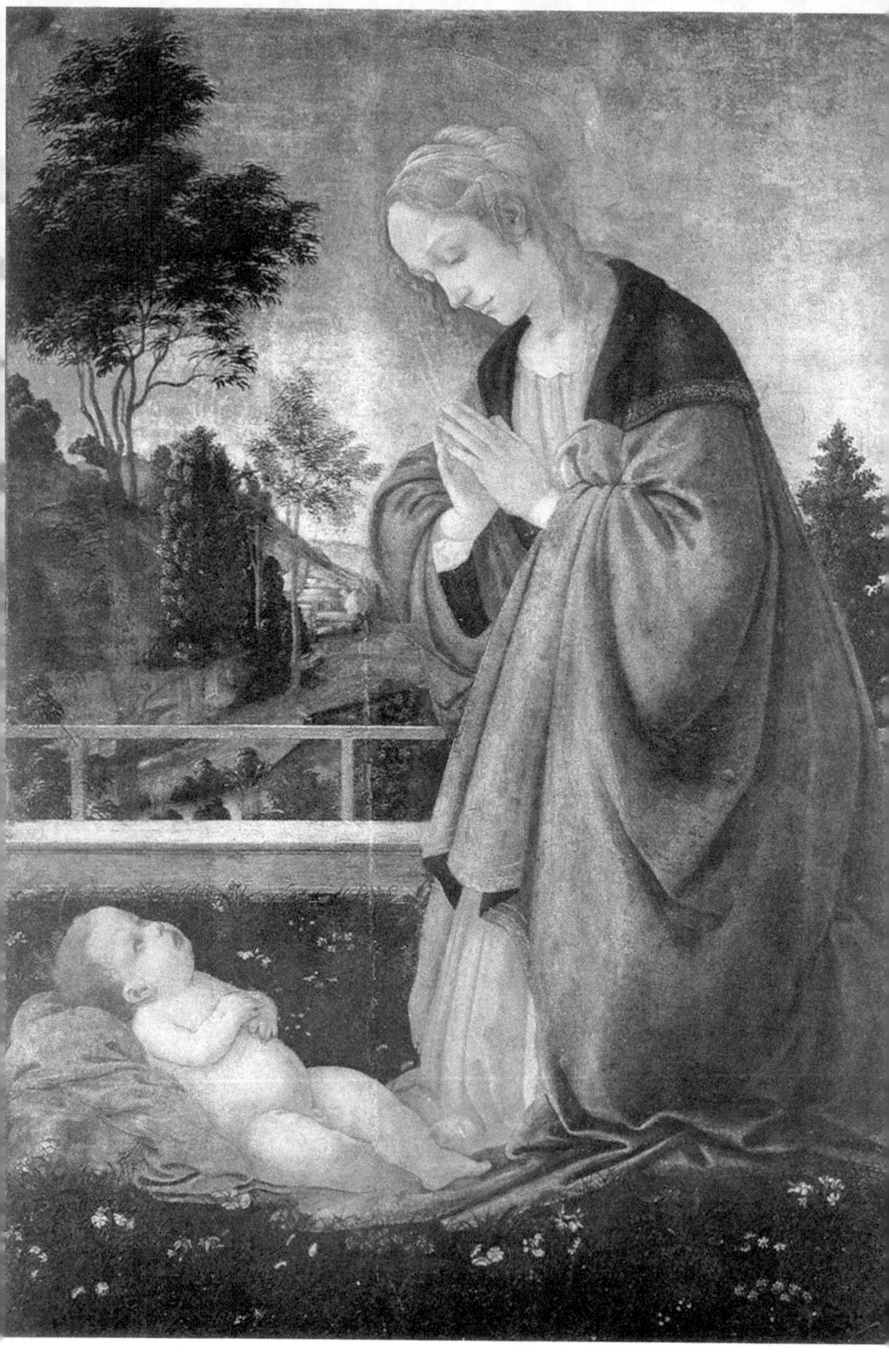

Filippino Lippi, The Adoration of the Child, c. 1483, Uffizi

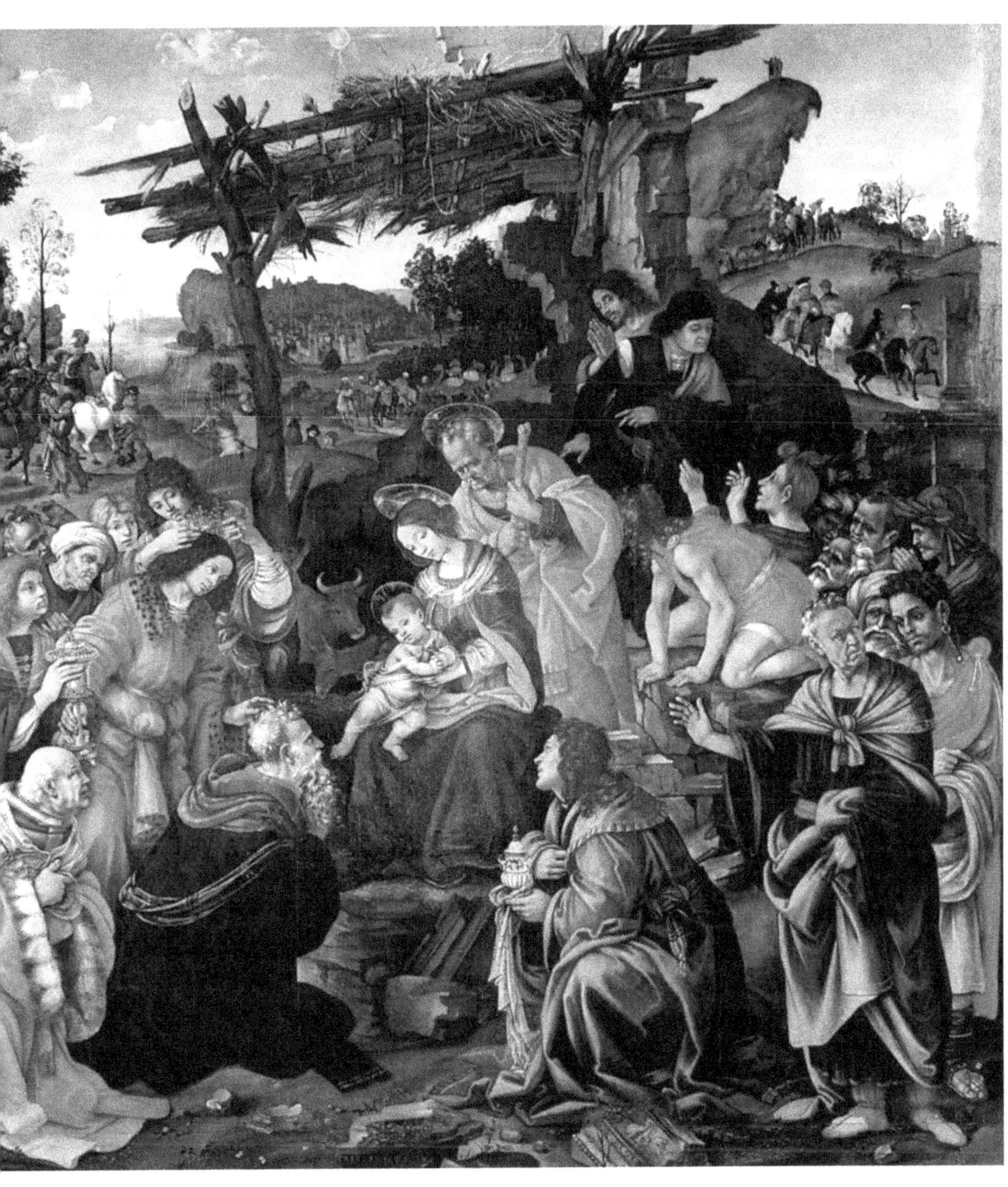

Filippino Lippi, The Adoration of the Magi, 1496, Uffizi

III

The Sant' Ambrogio altarpiece must have added enormously to the reputation which the Carmelite painter enjoyed among his contemporaries. It was only natural that he should have been chosen by the *proposto* Gemignano Inghirami and by the magistrates of Prato to undertake the fresco decoration in the choir of the cathedral of that city, when Fra Angelico, in spite of repeated urging, refused to accept this important commission, his time being fully occupied by the completion of the series of frescoes at the Vatican. In the spring of 1452, Fra Filippo, accompanied by his assistant, Fra Diamante, took up his abode at Prato, and entered upon the most eventful and artistically the most significant period of his career. As we have seen, he still kept up his workshop in Florence, where his temporary presence is repeatedly testified by documentary evidence during the next few years. Thus, although he began to work in the choir chapel immediately after his arrival at Prato, as may be seen from the entry in the *Libra delle spese* in the *Archivio del Patrimonio ecclesiastico* in Prato, recording under date of May 29, 1452, the payment of fifty lire to "Fra Diamante di Feo da Terranuova, gharzone di Fra Filippo di Tommaso," his frequent absence and general dilatoriness were the cause of so much delay that the decoration of the chapel was not completed before 1468, a year before the master's death.

During this period of sixteen years Fra Filippo continued to be employed by the members of the Medici family, by the *proposto* Gemignano Inghirami, and by many other patrons in Prato and Pistoja. In addition to his frequent absence in Florence, he no doubt undertook several other journeys, of one of which at least we have certain knowledge: his sojourn in 1461 at Perugia, whither he was called to value Bonfigli's frescoes in the Palazzo del Comune – an honourable task which devolved upon him as the sole survivor of the three artists chosen for it by the Signory of Perugia, the other two being Fra Angelico, who died in 1455, and Domenico Veneziano, whose death occurred in the spring of the very year that witnessed the completion of Bonfigli's frescoes.

But quite apart from such interruptions in the execution of that superb series of frescoes at Prato, depicting scenes from the lives of St. John the Baptist and St. Stephen, as were due to professional causes, there was enough excitement and disturbance in the artist's private life to account at least in part for his tardiness in completing the work which constitutes his greatest claim to immortal fame. For Prato was the scene of the great romance of Fra Filippo's life, by which his name has become familiar even to those who know little of, and care less about, his artistic achievement. The abduction of the nun, Lucrezia Buti, by the amorous monk, who was then entering upon the sixth decade of his life, is on the whole correctly recorded by Vasari, and has formed the subject of many a literary romance and pictorial rendering. Subsequent doubts thrown upon it by such eminent critics as, among others, Messrs. Crowe and Cavalcaselle, who maintain that the story rests upon the sole testimony of Vasari, and that "contingent circumstances tend to create considerable doubts of Vasari's truth," almost succeeded in relegating the amorous friar's daring exploit into the realm of fiction, until Milanesi's researches established the substantial truth of the romantic story. The facts, briefly stated, are as follows:

On the death of the Florentine silk merchant, Francesco Buti, in 1450, his son, Antonio, found himself charged with the responsibility of a not too profitable business, and a large family of twelve brothers and sisters. The eldest of these sisters, Margherita, was married off to Antonio Doffi in 1451, and in the same year two other sisters, Spinetta, born 1434, and Lucrezia, born 1435, were placed with the nuns of Sta. Margherita at Prato, Antonio paying the required fee of fifty florins for each of them. Needless to say, the two girls thus committed to a living tomb at the very time when life beckoned to them with all its joys and seductions, were not consulted in this matter any more than was Fra Filippo when, as a mere child, he had to enter the establishment of the Carmelites in Florence. Presumably the two lively, handsome girls had no more vocation for the cloistral life than the pleasure-loving friar - which circumstance may be pleaded in mitigation of the scandalous offence of which they subsequently became guilty.

Whether Fra Filippo had become acquainted with the Buti maidens before they entered the nunnery of Sta. Margherita, which was then in charge of the Abbess Bartolommea de' Bovacchiesi, it is impossible to say. Certain it is, on the other hand, that the Madonna of the Pitti *tondo,* painted in 1452, already bears the features of the model who, in other pictures, has been identified as Lucrezia Buti. From this it may be assumed that Fra Filippo, who came to Prato only a year after the two sisters, and who lived there in a house opposite the convent of Sta. Margherita, must have known Lucrezia at least four years before she sat to him for the "Madonna della Cintola" in 1456, the year of her abduction. It is quite possible that the love-struck monk used the influence of his powerful protectors to secure his appointment as chaplain of Sta. Margherita, so as to facilitate intercourse with the object of his affection and desire. Nor did his by no means untainted reputation and the papal stigma (*qui plurima et nefanda scelera perpetravit*) stand in the way of the coveted post being actually conferred upon him in the year 1456.

In the same year, as soon as he had entered upon his new duties, the Abbess of Sta. Margherita commissioned the new chaplain to paint an altarpiece for the high altar of the convent church. This afforded Fra Filippo a welcome opportunity for carrying out what must have been a carefully and cunningly devised scheme. He begged the Abbess to allow Lucrezia Buti, "who was exceedingly beautiful and graceful," to sit for the head of the Madonna; and, having obtained this favour, presumably did not fail to advance his cause. His clerical habit and the great difference of age between the monk and the nun – he was then about fifty, and Lucrezia twenty-one – may have helped to disarm suspicion: they did not prevent the young nun from taking the fatal step which was bound to bring disgrace and dishonour upon her; which, indeed, was accounted a crime, for Lucrezia was not, as Vasari has it, "either a novice or a boarder," but one of the eight "choral and professed nuns" who formed the establishment of Santa Margherita.

The plot came to a successful issue on the 1st of May 1456, during the celebration of the feast of the Madonna della Cintola – Our Lady of the Girdle. On that day it was the custom to exhibit at the Cathedral a sacred relic, purporting to be the miraculous girdle given to St. Thomas by the Virgin, who appeared to him after her death. That day was one of the rare occasions when the nuns of Sta. Margherita left the precincts of their convent to join the worshippers in the Duomo. On May 1, 1456, there were eight nuns who set out to pray before the sacred girdle – but seven only returned to the convent. Lucrezia Buti had been carried off by her monkish lover to his house; and if any attempts were made to induce her to return, either to Sta. Margherita, or to her relatives in Florence, she lent a deaf ear to these appeals. Vasari relates that "the father of Lucrezia was so grievously afflicted thereat, that he never more recovered his cheerfulness, and made every possible effort to regain his child." This, of course, is pure invention, since Francesco Buti had been mouldering in his grave for six years when the abduction took place.

And now we come to the most amazing chapter of this fifteenth-century romance. Fra Filippo Lippi, the monk who had broken his vow and was openly living at Prato with the equally guilty nun, actually continued to administer to the spiritual welfare of the nuns of the convent that had been so irretrievably disgraced by his conduct! That his misdeed was allowed to pass unpunished and uncensured, may have encouraged others to follow his and Lucrezia's example. Whether or not the Carmelite was instrumental in helping the other nuns to escape, the fact remains that before long Spinetta Buti had joined her sister in Filippo's house, whilst three other nuns deserted the convent to live in illicit union with their lovers. The unfortunate Abbess, Bartolommea de' Bovacchiesi, whose portrait is to be seen as kneeling donor in the so-called "Madonna della Cintola," now in the Municipal Palace at Prato, died of shame and grief before the year came to a close.

The remote resemblance of the figure of St. Margaret, on the extreme left of that picture, to Lucrezia Buti as she appears in authentic works by the master, in addition to the fact that the "Madonna della Cintola" was originally in the church of Sta. Margherita, has given colour to the theory that this is the very altarpiece which figures so prominently in the chief romance of Filippo Lippi's life. The same claim has been advanced for the "Nativity" (No. 1343) at the Louvre. Much as one would like to identify either the one or the other with the picture referred to by the chroniclers, if only for the sentimental interest that would be attached to it, neither of the two can be accepted as authentic works by our artist. The best recent expert opinion has ascribed the Paris panel in turn to Fra Diamante, Pesellino, Stefano da Zevio, and Baldovinetti, agreeing only on the one point, that it cannot be by Fra Filippo. As regards the "Madonna della Cintola," critical analysis of the picture can only lead to the conviction that from beginning to end it is inferior bottega work, with never a trace of the master's own brush, although it may well be based on a design by Fra Filippo. It is true, the time that elapsed between the placing of the commission for the Sta. Margherita altarpiece and the abduction of Lucrezia was so short, that the picture may have been only just begun and left to be finished by some other inferior painter. On the other hand, there is no reason for this assumption, since Filippo Lippo continued to be connected with the convent in his capacity of chaplain.

In the year following that memorable feast of the Sacred Girdle, Lucrezia presented the friar with a son, who was to become known to fame as Filippino Lippi. The house in which he was born bears a commemorative inscription put up by the citizens of Prato in 1869:

FILIPPO LIPPI
COMPRÒ E ABITÒ QUESTA CASA
QUANDO COLORIVA GLI STUPENDI
AFFRESCHI DEL DUOMO
E QUÌ NACQUE NEL MCCCCLIX FILIPPINO
PRECURSORE DI RAFFAELLO

"Filippo Lippi bought and inhabited this house when he painted the stupendous frescoes of the Cathedral, and here was born in 1459 (it should read 1457) Filippino, the precursor of Raphael."

If proof were needed that the escape of the other nuns was closely connected with the abduction of Lucrezia, it may be found in the fact that, when Lucrezia, for some unknown reason, found it advisable to feign repentance and to return to the convent of Sta. Margherita at the end of 1458, all the other fugitives followed her example. They had to submit to the formality of twelve months' probation before they took the veil again, in a solemn ceremony, in December 1459. Perhaps the reason for Lucrezia's return is not altogether dissociated from the financial troubles that beset her lover, as we have seen, about the time of Filippino's birth. The sincerity of her renewed vow of chastity is to be gathered not only from the fact that in 1465 she presented Fra Filippo with another child – a daughter, who was given the name Alessandra – but in the clear indictment set forth by an anonymous accuser in a *tamburazione* under date of May 8, 1461. In this *tamburazione,* or secret accusation, addressed to the "officers of the night and monasteries of the city of Florence," a pretty state of affairs is revealed at the convent of Sta. Margherita, which "has been frequented and continues to be frequented by Ser Piero d'Antonio di Ser Vannozzo," who has "begot a male child in the said convent.... And if you wish to find him, you will find him every day in the convent, together with another man called frate Filippo. The latter excuses himself by saying that he is the chaplain, whilst the former says he is the procurator. And the said frate Filippo has had a male child by one called Spinetta. And he has in his house the said child, who is grown up and is called Filippino."

The anonymous accuser, of course, was mistaken in mentioning Spinetta, instead of her sister, as the mother of Filippino, who in his will expressly refers to "domine Lucretie ejus delicte matris et filie olim Francisci de Butis de Florentia," and thus removes every possible doubt as to his parentage. The mistake finds an easy explanation in the fact that both the sisters were for some time under Fra Filippo's roof.

What was the end of Lippi's romance? There are no contemporary records to throw clear light upon it. In Milanesi's edition of Vasari it is stated that Pope Eugene granted the monk a special dispensation to marry Lucrezia. If any such dispensation ever was granted, it must have been by Pius II., and not by Eugene. Under any circumstances, it seems very improbable that Fra Filippo, as we learn from the same source, should have refused to avail himself of this permission to legalise his union, because "he preferred to continue living the sort of life that pleased him." He was then a man of considerable age, near the end of his life, and past the times for "sowing his wild oats." The papal dispensation, if actually given, must have been sought for, in which case Filippo would presumably have availed himself of it; or, if granted on the Pope's own initiative, could not have been lightly set aside by a humble member of the Church, who was largely dependent on the emoluments accruing from his clerical appointments. The mere fact that Lucrezia's features are to be recognised in the friar's latest works, the frescoes in the Cathedral of Spoleto, tends to prove that the old man's affection was not transferred to different quarters; and Vasari's suggestion that his death was due to the libertinism of his conduct, which led to his being poisoned by certain relatives of a woman with whom he had become entangled, may be dismissed as a fable.

Vasari is at fault again in ascribing the commission for the decoration of the chapel in the Church of Our Lady at Spoleto, Fra Filippo's last important work, to the influence of Cosimo de' Medici. Fra Filippo went to Spoleto in 1467, and Cosimo had been buried in 1464. If any member of the Medici family had acted as mediator, it must have been Piero, who had always been a patron and protector of our artist. Of the four frescoes at Spoleto illustrating the Life of the Virgin, only the "Coronation" and the "Annunciation" are, so far as one can judge in their much restored condition, from the master's own hand. "The Death of the Virgin" and the "Nativity," though undoubtedly designed by him, are vastly inferior in execution, and are almost entirely the work of his assistant, Fra Diamante, who accompanied him to Spoleto, and stayed there several months after his master's death to complete the unfinished work.

Fra Filippo died on the 9th of October 1469, and left his son Filippino under the guardianship of Fra Diamante. He was buried in the church which had witnessed his last labours. The esteem in which he was held by those who knew how to appreciate his art - and among them, surely, the Medici must be placed at the top - found expression in the rivalry between Florence and Spoleto over his remains. When Lorenzo the Magnificent, some years after the great Carmelite's death, passed through Spoleto as ambassador of the Florentine Commonwealth, he demanded Fra Filippo's body from the Spoletans, for re-interment in the Duomo of Florence. The Spoletans' reply is characteristic of the spirit of the age: they begged to be left in possession of the remains of the master, since they were so poorly provided with distinguished men, whereas Florence had enough and to spare. Lorenzo must have been touched by a request presented in such flattering terms, for he not only allowed Filippo Lippi's body to remain in its original resting-place, but he commissioned from Filippino Lippi, the inheritor of the monk's artistic genius, a marble tomb, on which can be seen to this day the jovial features of the master thus honoured, the arms of Lorenzo and of the Lippi, and the commemorative inscription composed by the great humanist, Angelo Poliziano.

> CONDITVS HIC EGO SVM PICTVRE FAMA PHILIPPVS
> NVLLI IGNOTA MEÆ EST GRATIA MIRA MANVS;
> ARTIFICIS POTVI DIGITIS ANIMARE COLORES
> SPERATAQVE ANIMOS FALLERE VOCE DIV:
> IPSA MEIS STVPVIT NATVRA EXPRESSA FIGVRIS
> MEQVE SVIS FASSA EST ARTIBVS ESSE PAREM.
> MARMOREO TVMVLO MEDICES LAVRENTIVS HIC ME
> CONDIDIT, ANTE HVMILI PVLVERE TECTVS ERAM.

IV

It is not within the scope of this brief sketch of the life and art of Fra Filippo Lippi to enter into a detailed critical discussion of his extant works. I am not here concerned with questions of debatable attributions, or with the share that Fra Diamante and other assistants or pupils may have had in the execution of works that pass generally under his name. All that can here be attempted is, to gather from the cumulative evidence of the pictures that are unquestionably by the master's own hand, the real significance of his great achievement and the place he occupies in the evolution of Italian art. In the progress of his style from the early "Nativities" to the Prato frescoes is reflected the whole course of Early Renaissance art from Gothic awkwardness to full freedom. Of course, Fra Filippo lived in a period of transition and of passionate striving for expression; and to a certain extent every artist is the product of the spirit of his time. The tendencies which resulted in the full blossoming of Renaissance art were at work, and would, no doubt, have conquered in the end, even if Filippo Lippi had never existed. Nevertheless, he was one of the greatest initiators of the Renaissance in painting; and it is his peculiar merit that, at a period of artistic pupilage, when every painter's training was directed towards the close assimilation of his particular master's peculiarities, and when progress consisted largely in the grafting of some personal note or other on to the inherited tradition, Fra Filippo not only liberated himself from the narrow confines of his early training by his readiness to benefit from the example of any native or "foreign" master who had added some new word to the language of art, but he was also ever ready to learn direct from the greatest source of artistic inspiration – from Nature.

From his earliest beginnings, which rather suggest illuminated miniatures on a large scale, we see him grow step by step, acquire knowledge of perspective, of design, of colour harmonies, of the effect of light and atmosphere, of movement. We find him initiating advance in many directions. The circular composition, which was scarcely known before his days, is carried by him to such perfection, that it becomes the favourite device of most later Florentine painters. He is the first Florentine who shows a real appreciation of the beauty of Nature, who allows real daylight to enter into his pictures, and who studies reflections. The Florentine School was never a school of *painters* in the strict sense of the word, like the Venetian School. Its work was always based on linear design, upon which colour was superadded – an afterthought, as it were. The Florentine did not think in terms of colour. But Fra Filippo, without abandoning the essentially Florentine insistence on linear design, came nearer the true pictorial conception than any of his contemporaries or successors. In his first "Nativity" at the Florentine Academy he gives not the slightest hint of the astounding development his art was to undergo before he left Florence for Prato. The colour is purely localised, like the flat tones of the Gothic miniaturists in whose school he had been trained. The Madonna looks as if she were cut out and pasted on to the landscape. What a step from its hard delineation to the *morbidezza,* and the cool shimmering tones and all-pervading sense of atmosphere in his "Coronation of the Virgin," which, in this respect, remains a unique achievement in Florentine art. Both his Florentine "Nativities" are as awkward and clumsy in design as could be. Lopped-off figures of praying monks are squeezed into the extreme corners; the landscape background is seen in steep perspective, almost as in a bird's-eye view, and has no relation to the figures in the foreground; the perspective and the whole arrangement of the ruined building in the one are childish. And a few years later he had arrived at the noble architectonic design of the "Virgin Enthroned," at the Louvre, in which, notwithstanding here and there a reminiscence of Gothic awkwardness, the figure of the angel on the left foreshadows the easy grace of similarly poised figures in Andrea del Sarto's art.

Again and again Fra Filippo acts as initiator and sets the fashion for whole generations of artists. He is one of the first to experiment with devices for producing the illusion of depth, either by the interpolation, between the foreground and the background figures, of architectural elements, as in the Louvre "Madonna" - the idea had already served Donatello in the sister-art of sculpture - or by the skilful disposition and lighting of the subsidiary figures in the background, as in the episodes from the life of St. Anne, which form the setting to the adorable "Madonna and Child" of the Pitti *tondo.* If Michelangelo's nude athletes in the background of his "Holy Family" *tondo* are based upon the similar figures in Luca Signorelli's circular "Madonna and Child" at the Uffizi, Signorelli himself clearly derived from Filippo Lippi the use of the background figures, one of whom turns his back to the spectator just like the women on the extreme right of Lippi's *tondo,* for the purpose of enhancing the sense of depth and space. This woman with the boy clinging to the folds of her dress, as well as the one by whom she is preceded - a rapidly moving figure, with clinging diaphanous garments and with a basket poised on her head - will be found again and again during the next half-century of Florentine art, just as the Uffizi "Madonna adoring the Divine Child," who is supported by two boy-angels, became the prototype of a long succession of similar pictures. In the dancing "Salome" of the Prato frescoes, again, we have the forerunner of the type of figure and movement that received its highest development in the art of Botticelli, Filippo Lippi's greatest pupil.

Every phase of the triumphant progress of Renaissance art finds an echo in Filippo Lippi's painting. Masaccio helped him to shake off Gothic awkwardness and to achieve a certain degree of statuesque dignity. From Gentile da Fabriano he took the delight in gay, festive attire and sumptuous pageantry, which is clearly expressed in Sir Frederick Cook's *tondo,* and in a modified form in the Academy "Coronation." Pier dei Franceschi's great conquest of the realm of light and air did no more fail to leave its mark upon the Carmelite's art, than did Paolo Uccello's discoveries in the science of perspective. The classic thrones of his Madonnas and the architectural backgrounds of some of his pictures proclaim his enthusiasm for the forms and decorative details of the Renaissance churches and palaces that were then rising, under the influence of the new learning, in every part of Florence. Nor is it possible to over-estimate the prodigious effect produced upon the artist-monk's receptive mind by his study of the works of Donatello. The Uffizi "Madonna" is in reality a relief by Donatello or one of his followers translated into paint. Take any photographic reproduction of that picture, and examine the head of the roguishly smiling angel, the arms of the Infant Saviour and of the Madonna, and the way the whole group is set against the window-frame. The illusion is extraordinary. If it were not for the landscape seen through the opening in the background and the transparent folds of the veil over the Virgin's head, it would be pardonable to mistake the picture thus reduced to black and white for a bas-relief of the Donatello School.

Thus, with the shrewd intelligence of which his features in the auto-portrait introduced into the "Coronation" are so eloquent, Fra Filippo knew how to take hints and suggestions from the art of all his great contemporaries. But he applied the same keen intelligence to the study of the living world around him. The knowledge imparted to him by other masters was thus allowed to filter through his personal observation of Nature. And whilst it is possible to trace in his work the most varied artistic influences, his own personality was never eclipsed or obscured. Always ready to learn and to assimilate new principles, he never stooped to the imitation of mere mannerisms. From any such inclination he was saved by his temperament, his human sympathy, his artistic curiosity. Only to his earliest Madonnas cling reminiscences of Giottesque types and formulas. Even before he had reached full maturity, the typical had become ousted by the individual. And in this respect he was again an initiator in Florentine art. He was one of the first painters of his school who makes us feel that almost every character in his pictures is the result of personal observation - is practically a portrait. He is the first true genre painter of his school. Benozzo Gozzoli, it is true, went far beyond him as a pictorial raconteur of Florentine fifteenth-century life; but the origin of Benozzo's genre-like treatment of scriptural incidents, which makes his frescoes at Pisa and San Gimignano such precious documents, is to be found in Fra Filippo Lippi.

The Prato frescoes introduce several delicious incidents of this nature, like the leave-taking of St. John from his parents, or the child-birth scene in the episode in the life of St. Stephen. But they are not absent either from his altarpieces. The exquisitely recorded happenings in the house of St. Anne, which form the background of the Pitti "Madonna and Child," are pure genre-painting, and are, moreover, a daring departure from all the earlier conventions which ruled the rendering of this favourite subject. The earlier "Coronation of the Virgin" shows something of the same tendency in the charming group of a female saint and two children in front of the kneeling monk. The saint, like the Virgin Mary herself, is just an elegantly attired Florentine lady of the period. The very angels surrounding the throne of the Heavenly Father are humanised, as it were, by being divested of their wings. Even in the stately and formal "Virgin Enthroned," at the Louvre, Fra Filippo could not resist the temptation to introduce a roguish urchin on each side peeping over the balustrade, and thus transferring the scene from the heavenly region to this earth.

Fra Filippo loved the world in which he found so much beauty. For all that, his art reveals neither sensuality nor worldliness. He was indeed, as Mr. Berenson so happily describes him, a genre-painter, whose genre was that of the soul, as that of others was of the body. But he expressed the soul through the body. As M. André Maurel has it: "Before painting faces, he looked at them, which was a new thing.... He was a great painter, because he was a man."

On the following pages are some illustrations of contemporaries of Fra Filippo Lippi.

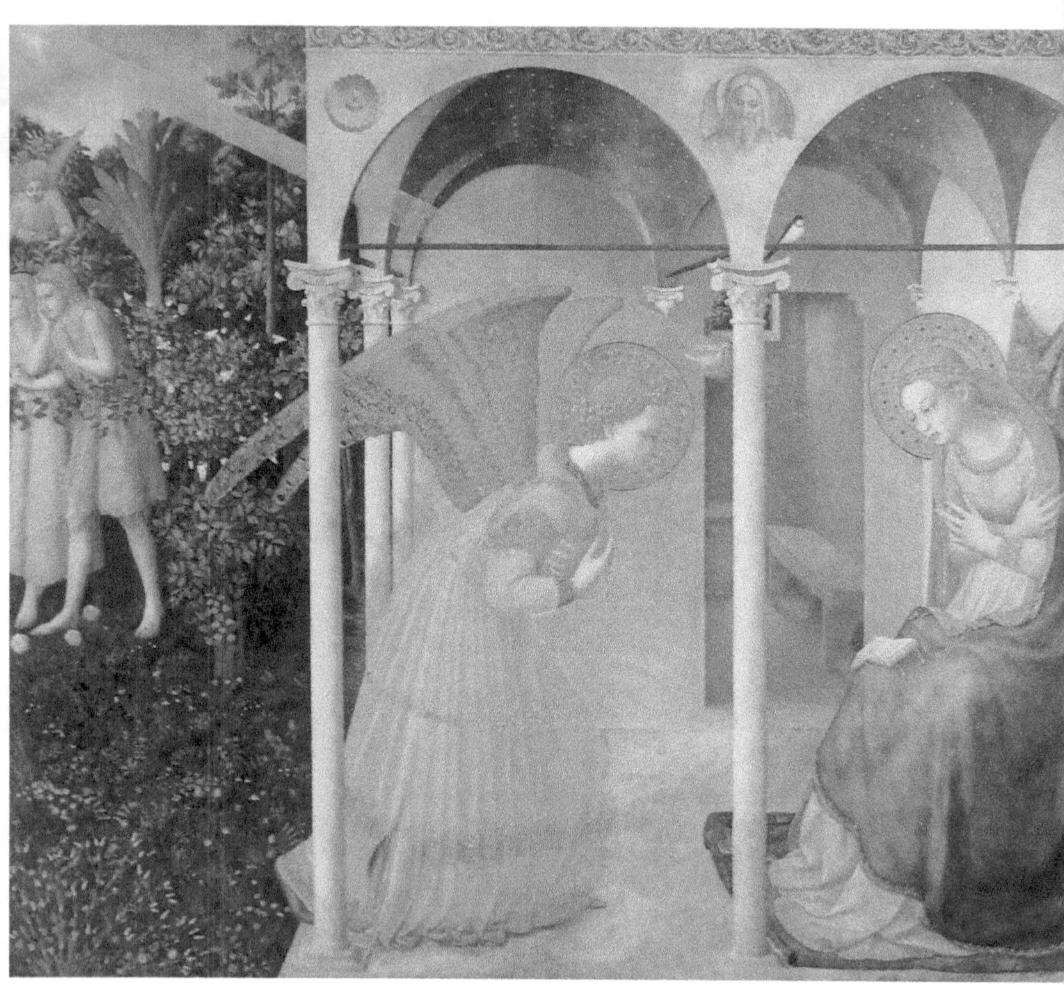

Fra Angelico, Annunciation, Prado, Madrid

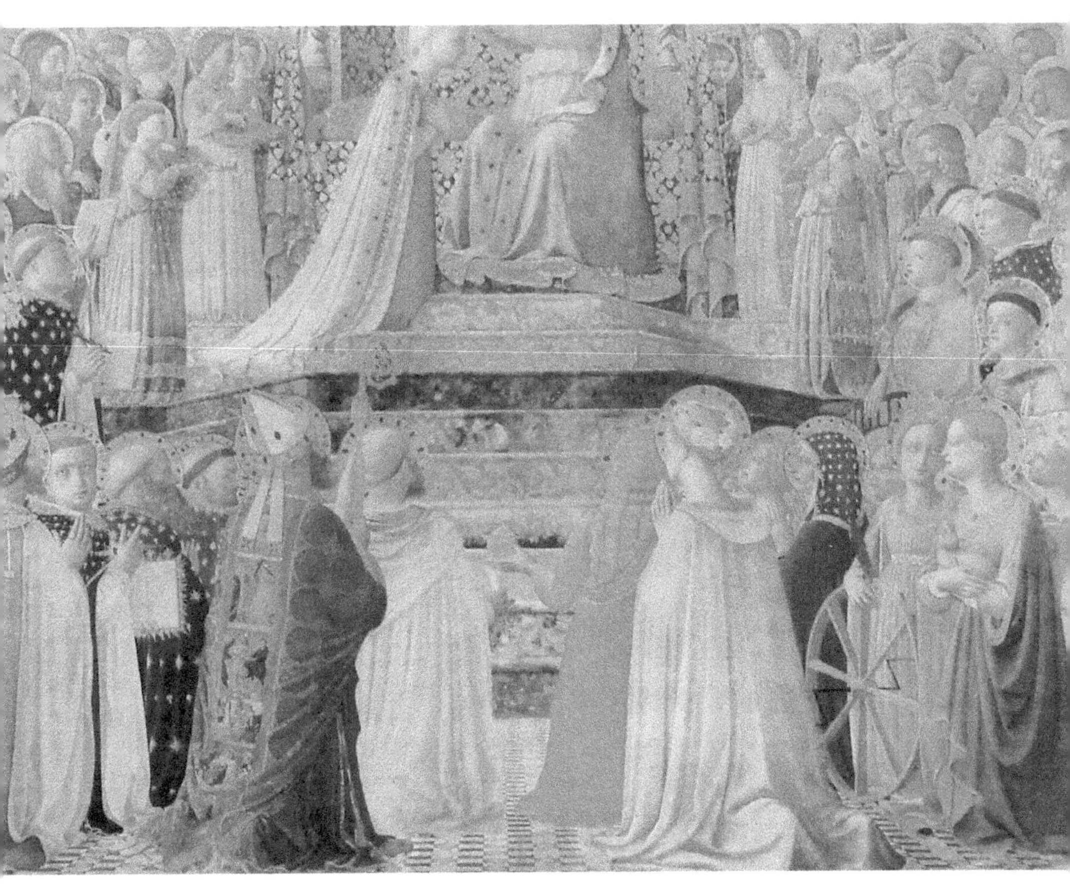

Fra Angelico, The Coronation of the Virgin, Louve, Paris, detail

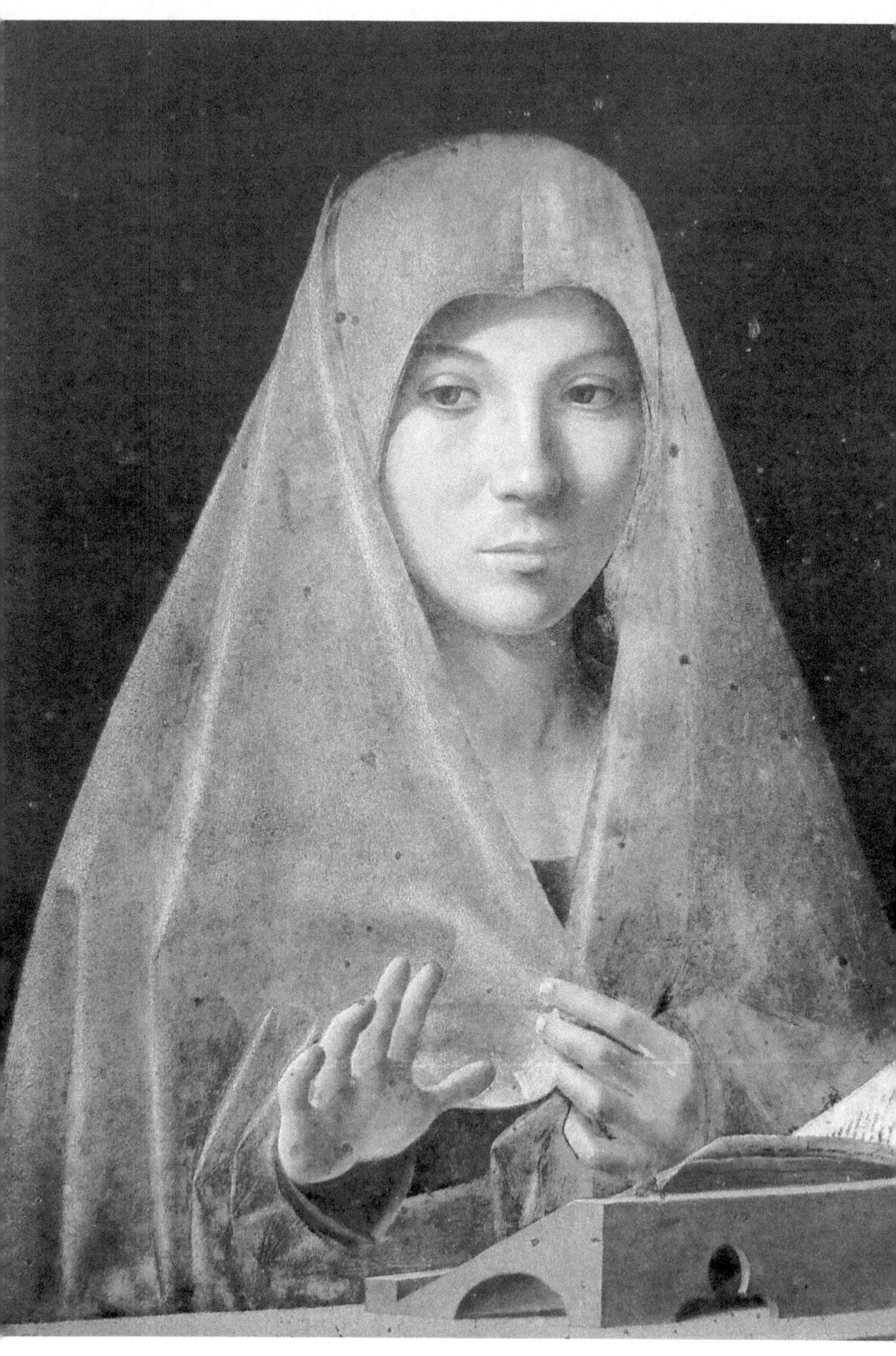

Antonello da Messina, The Virgin of the Annunciation, 1475, Palermo

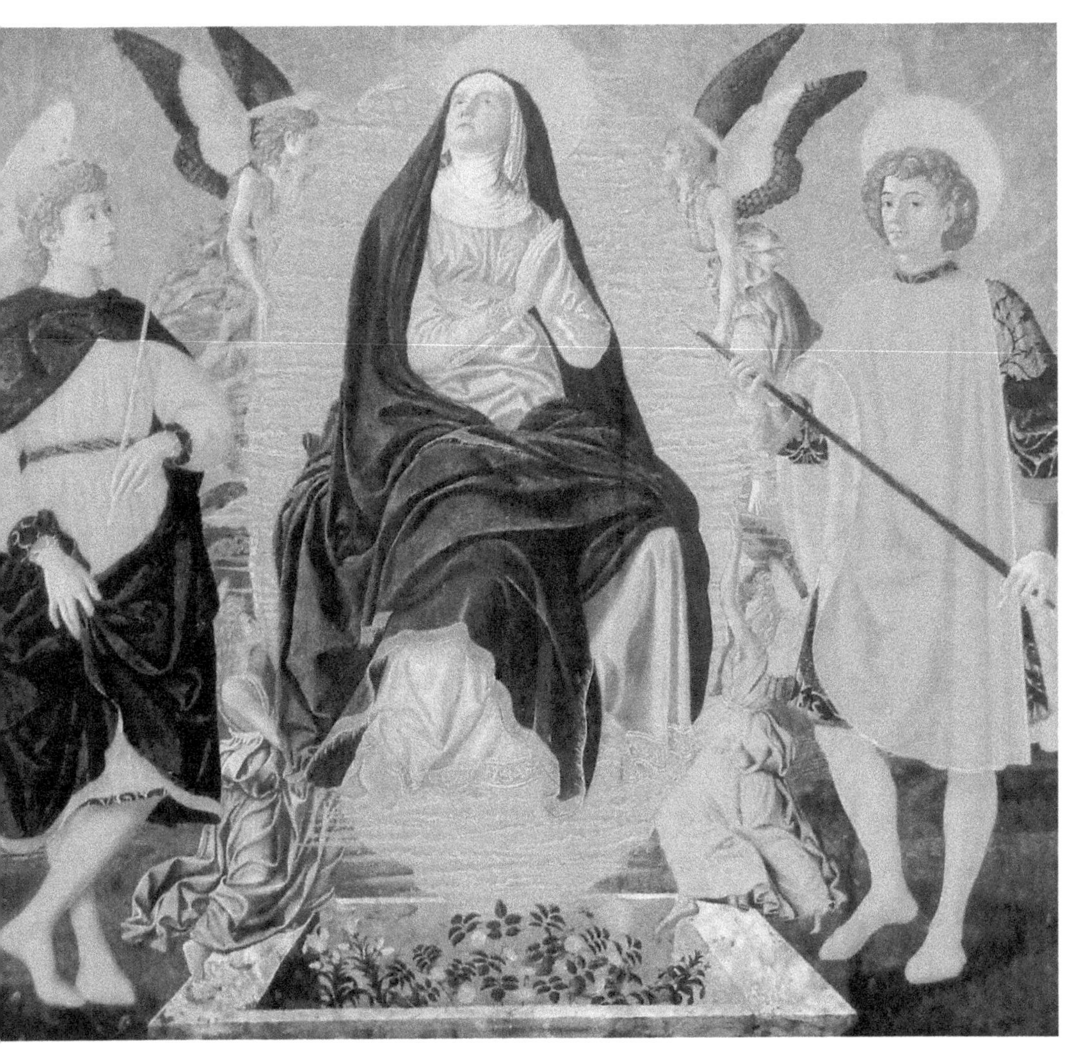

Andrea del Castagno, Assumption, Berlin

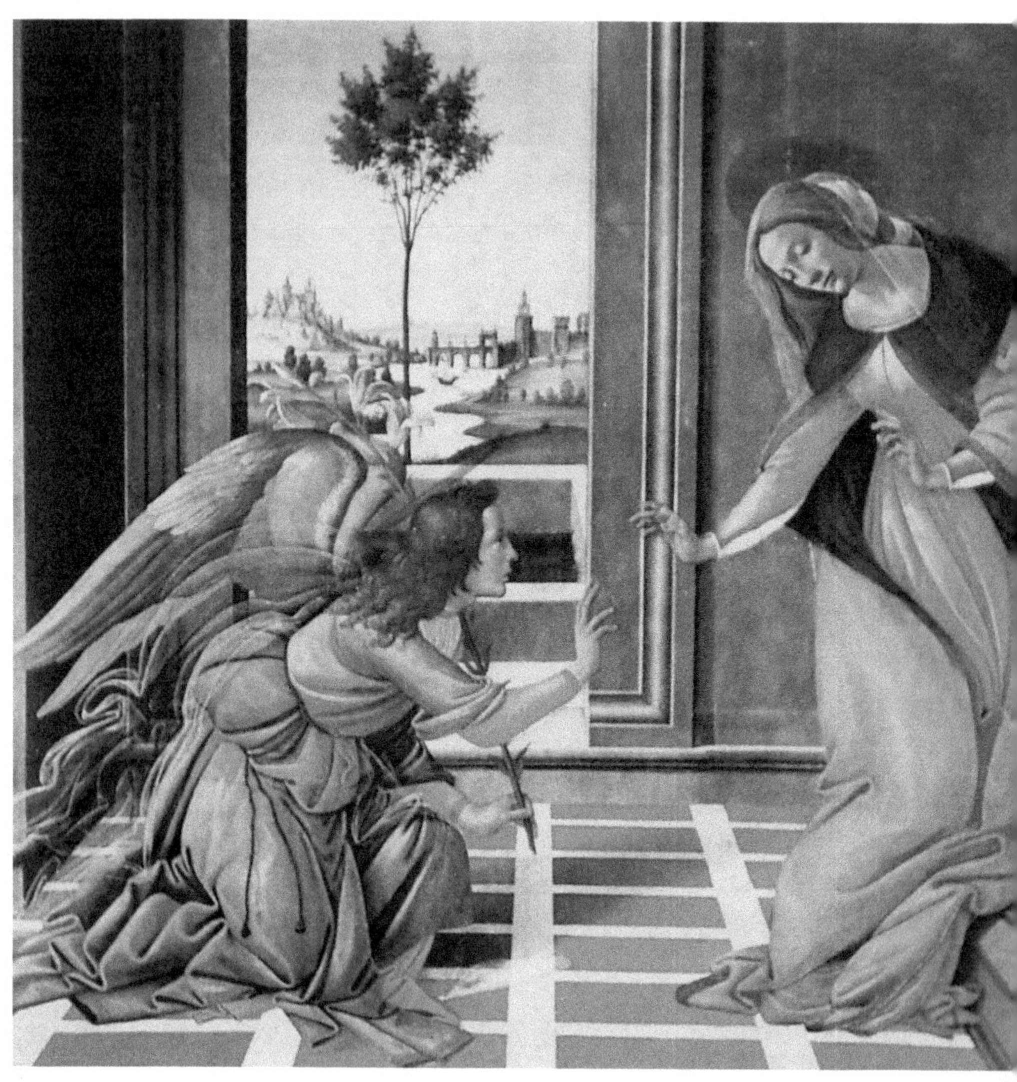

Sandro Botticelli, The Annunciation, Uffizi Gallery, Florence

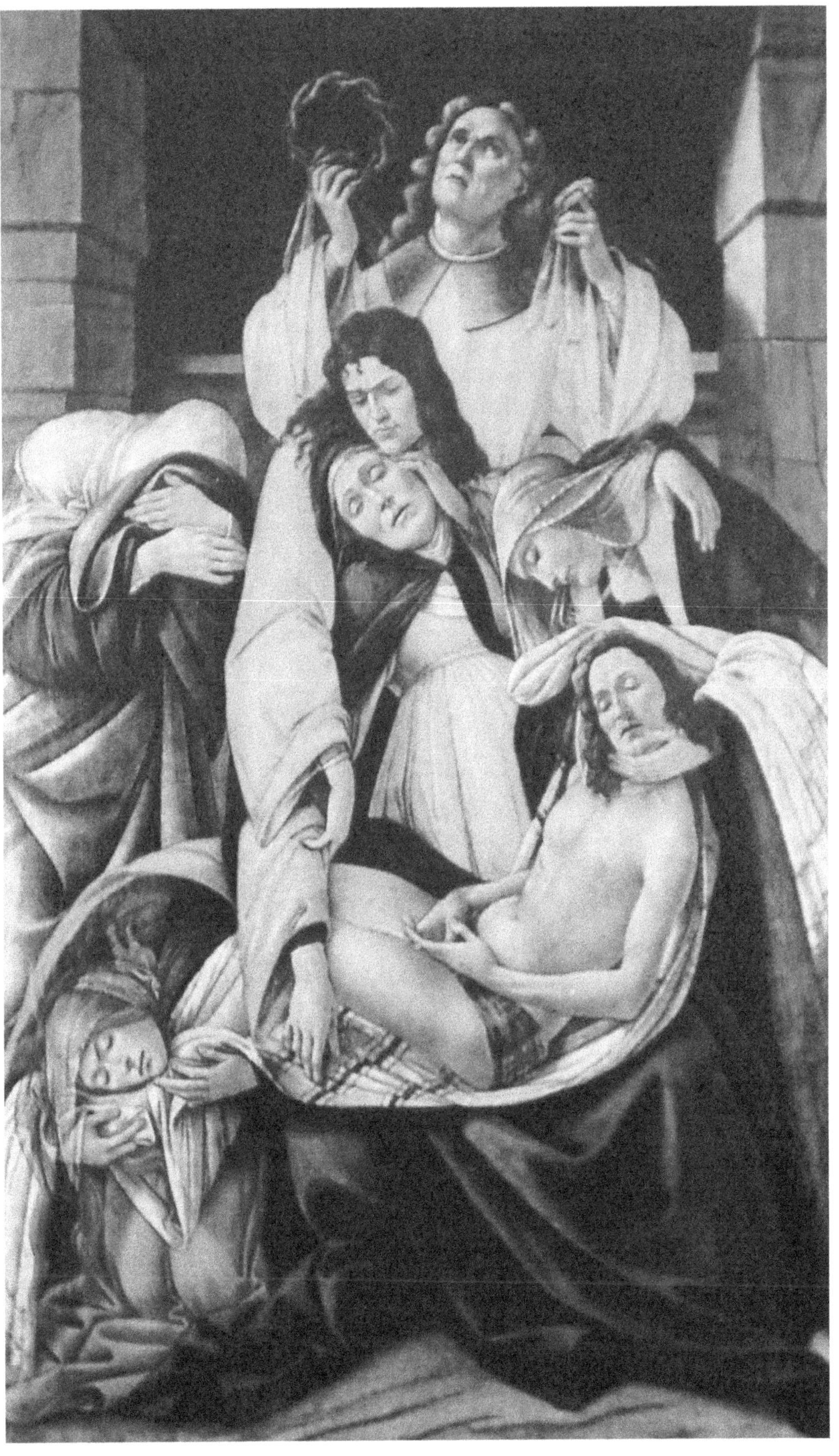

Sandro Botticelli, Pietà, Milan

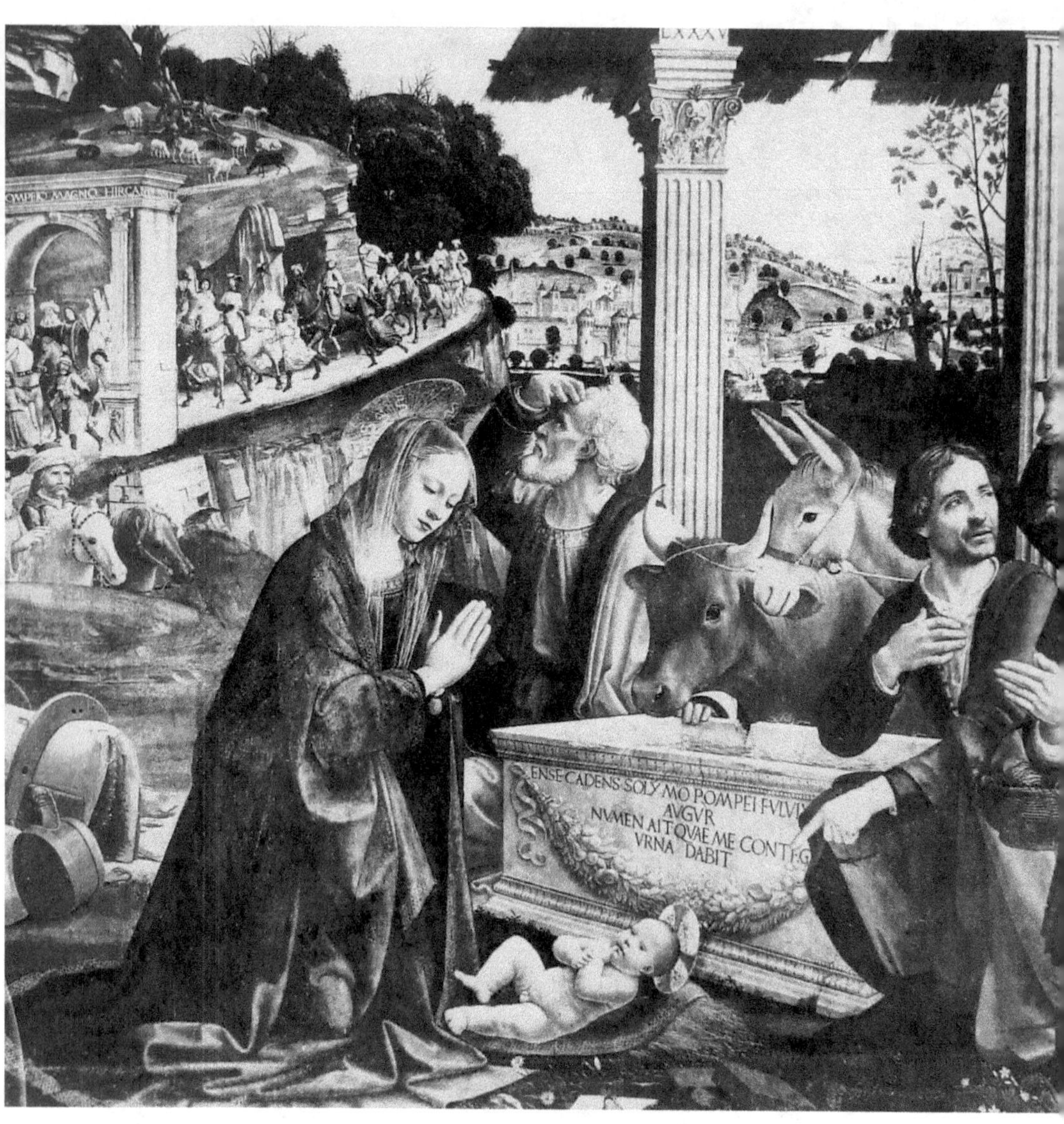

Domenico Ghirlandaio, Adoration of the Shepherds, 1485

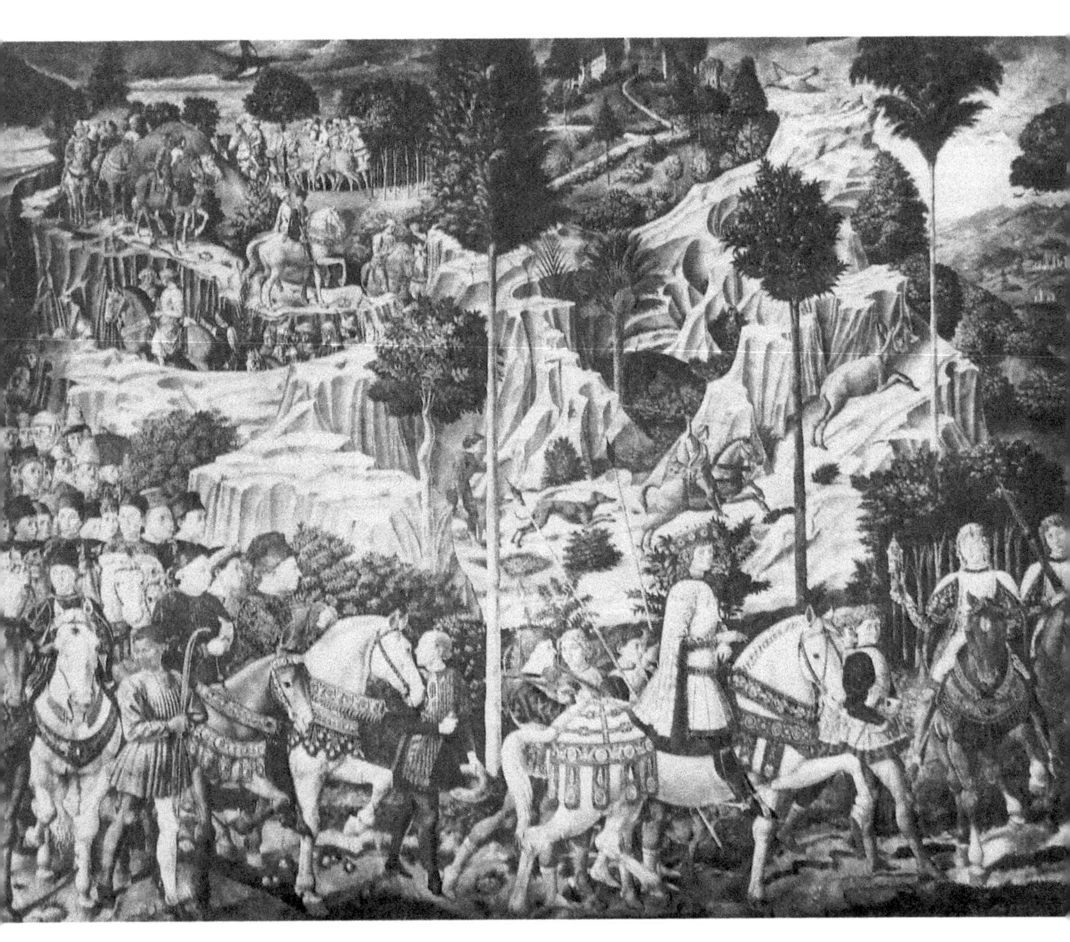

Benozzo Gozzoli, Journey of the Magi

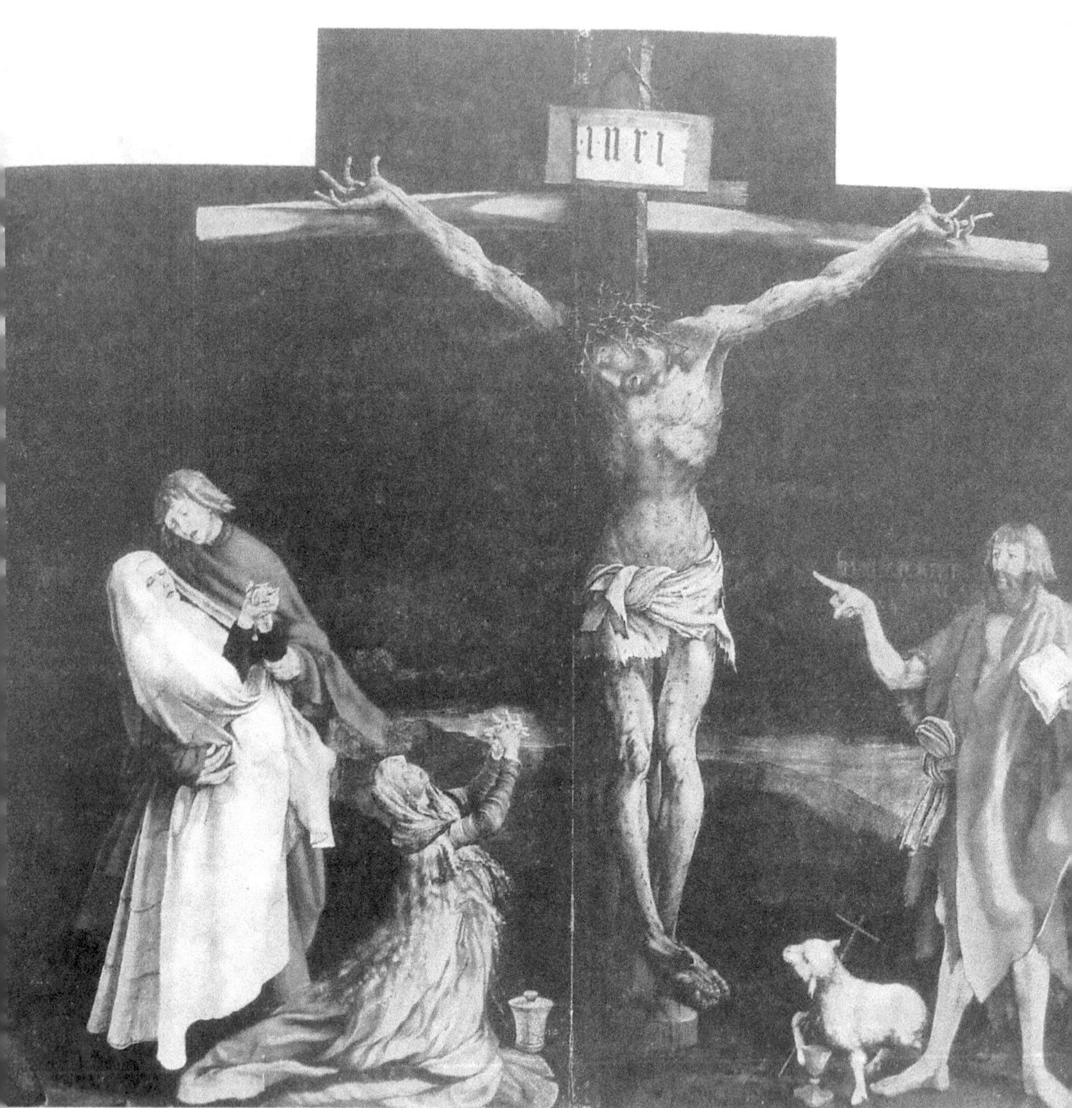

Matthias Grünewald, Crucifixion, Isenheim Altarpiece

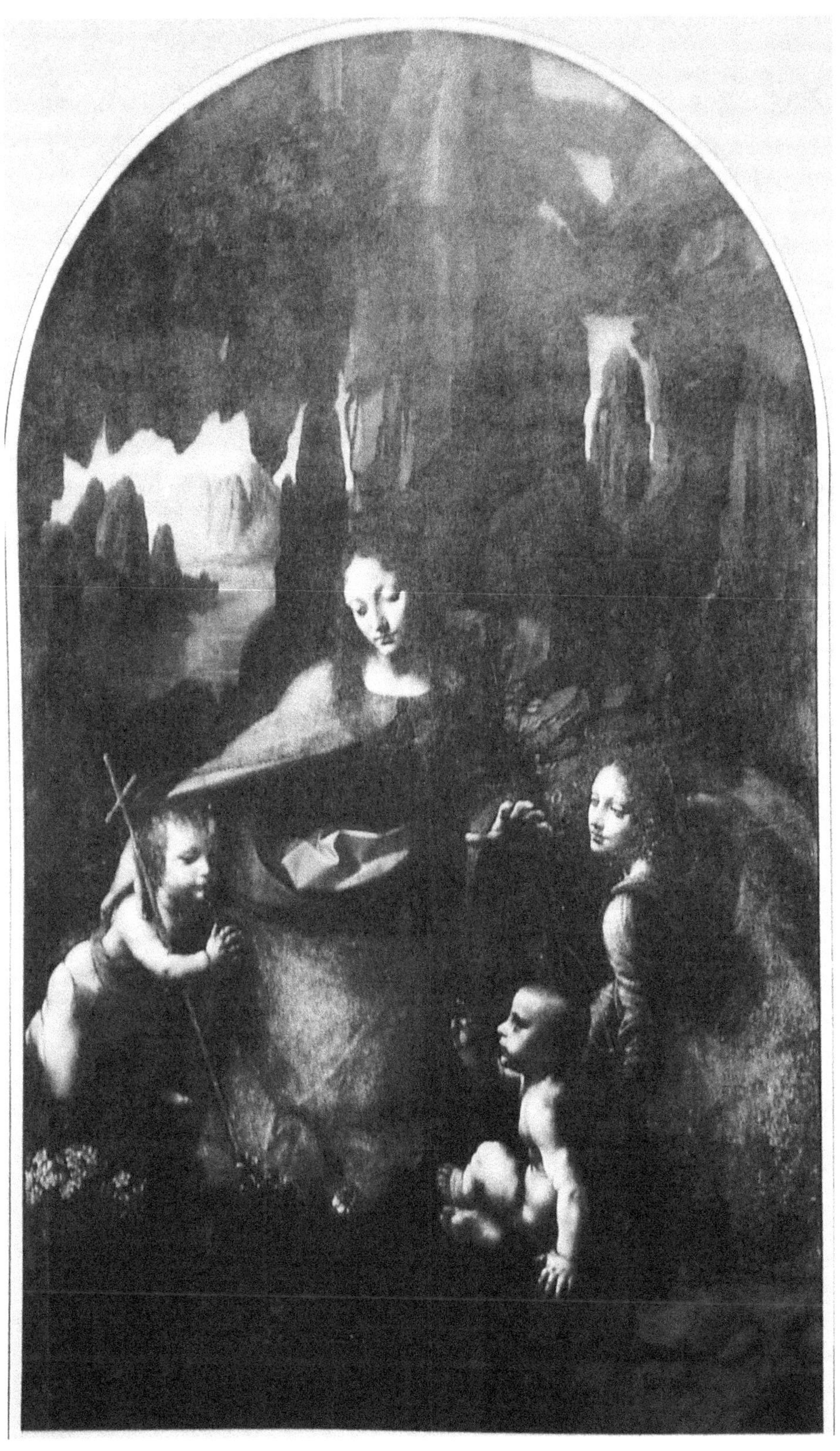

Leonardo da Vinci, The Madonna of the Rocks, London

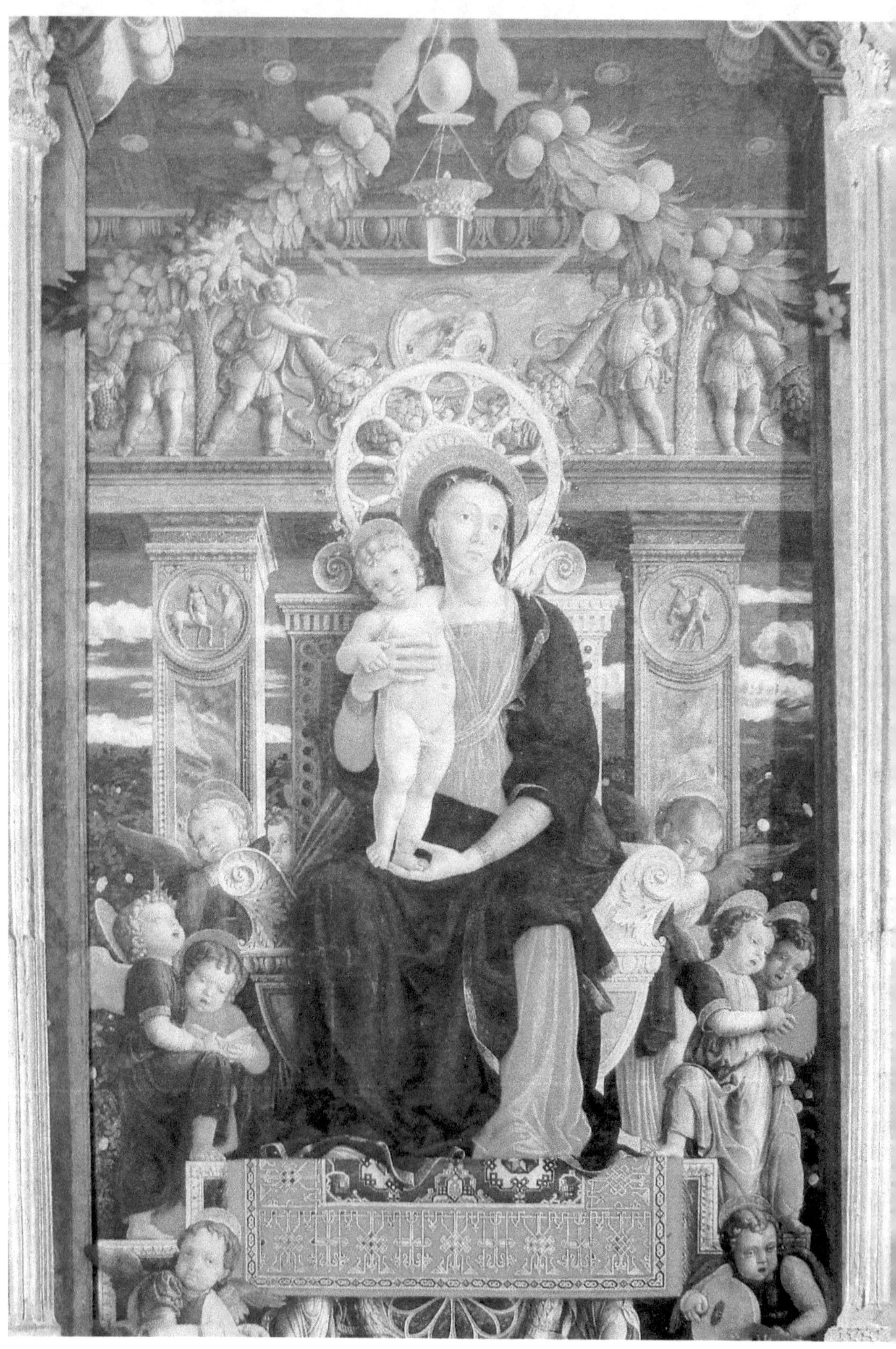

Andreas Mantegna, Madonna and Child Enthroned, 1457-60, Verona

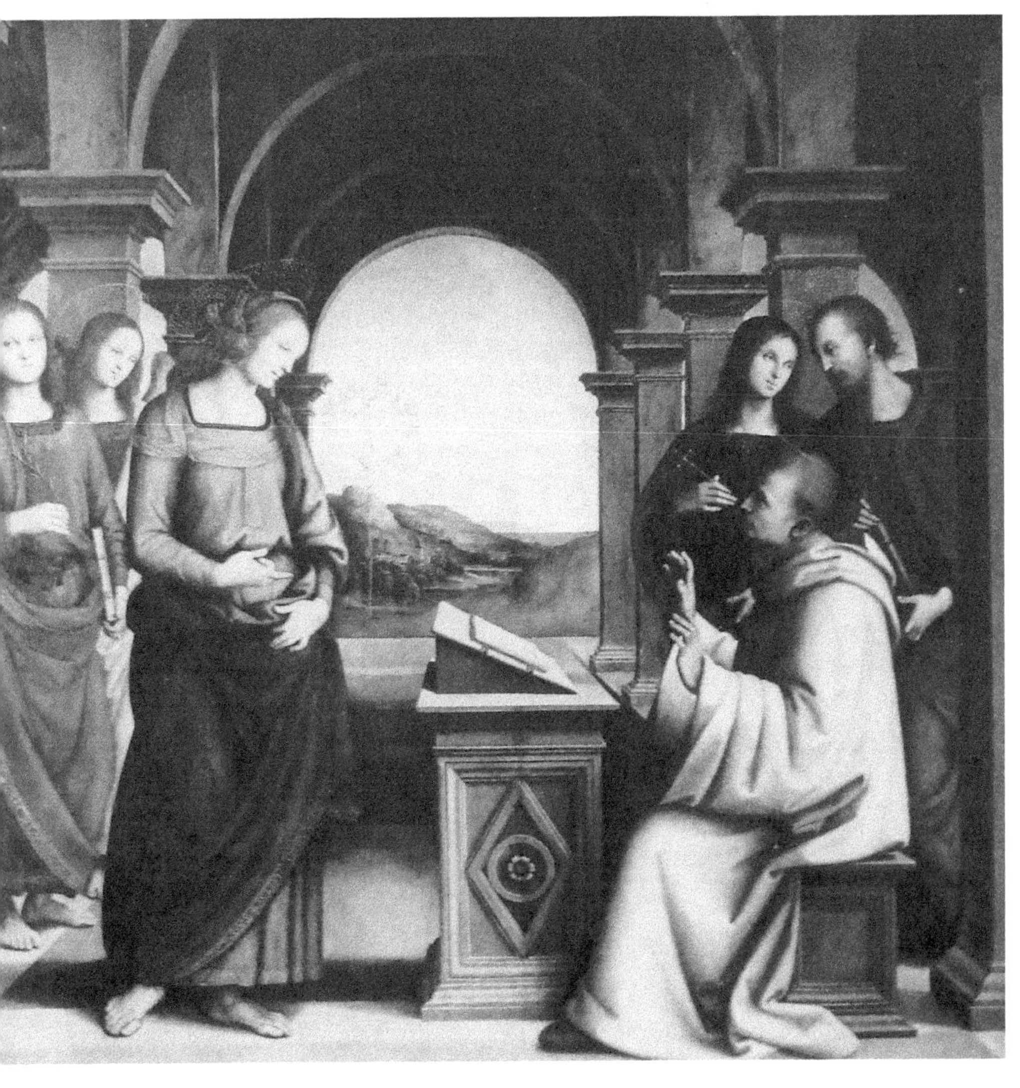

Perugino, Vision of St Bernard, 1488

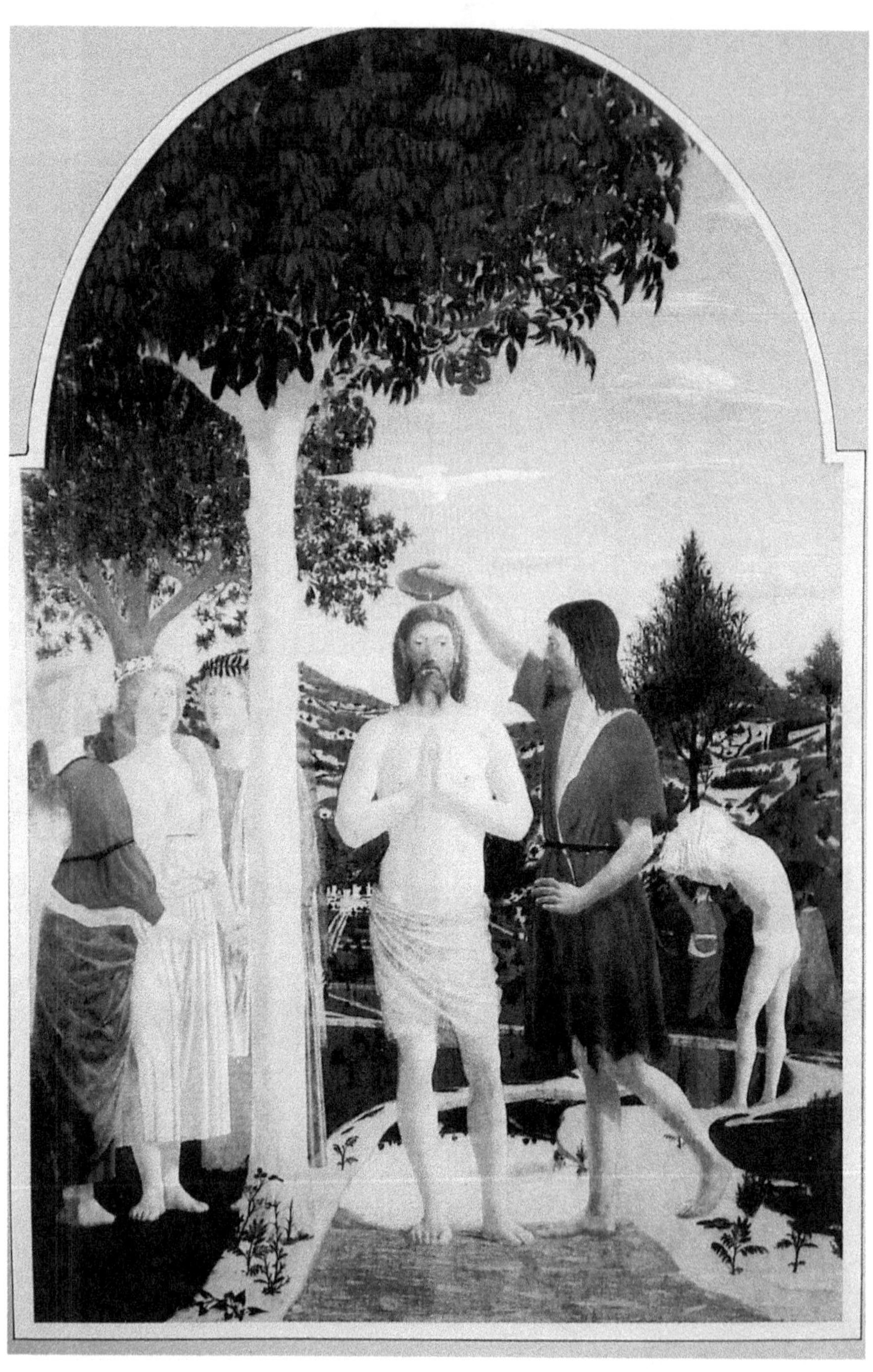

Piero della Francesca, *The Baptism of Christ*, National Gallery, London

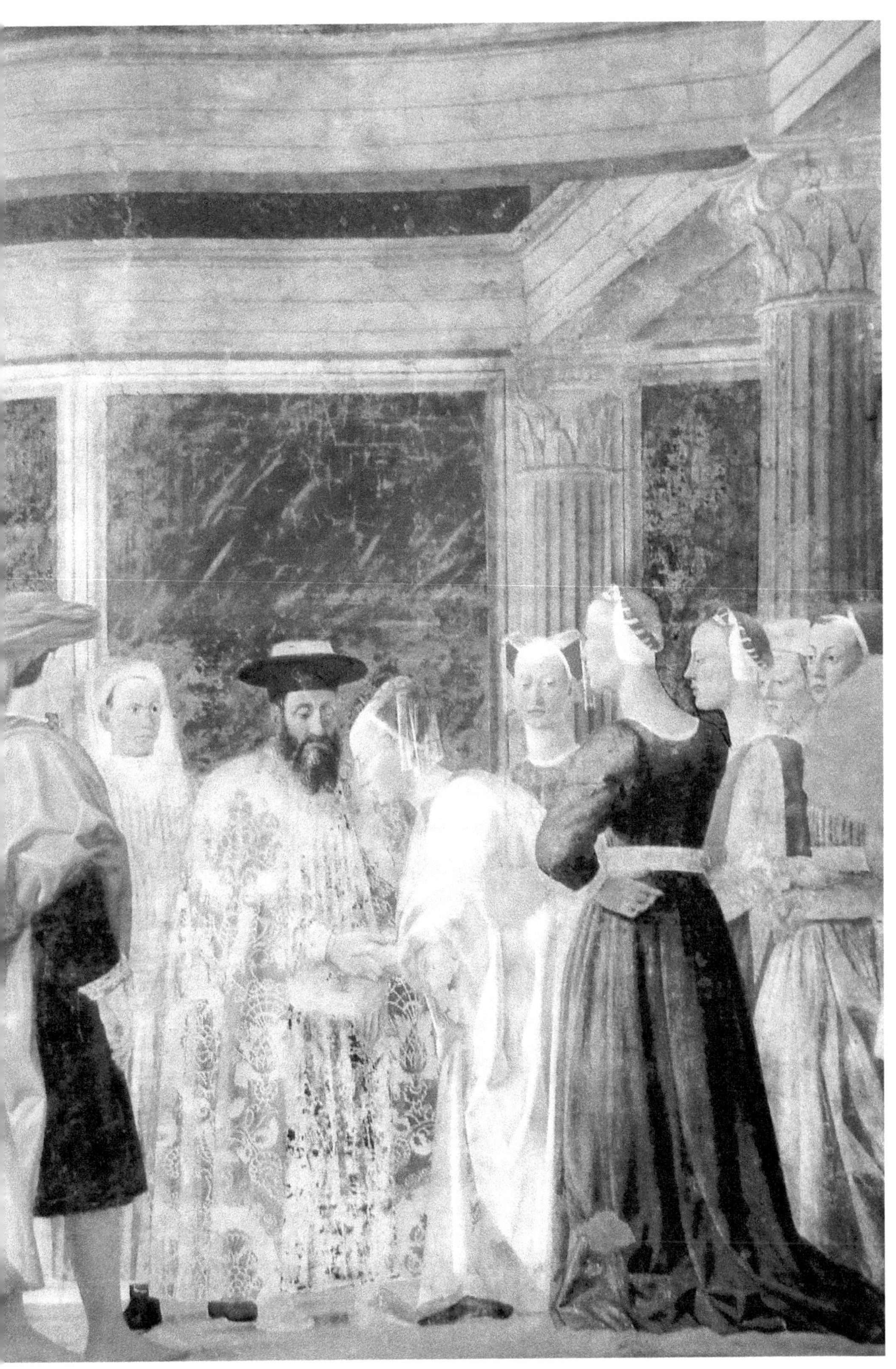

Piero della Francesca, frescoes, Arezzo

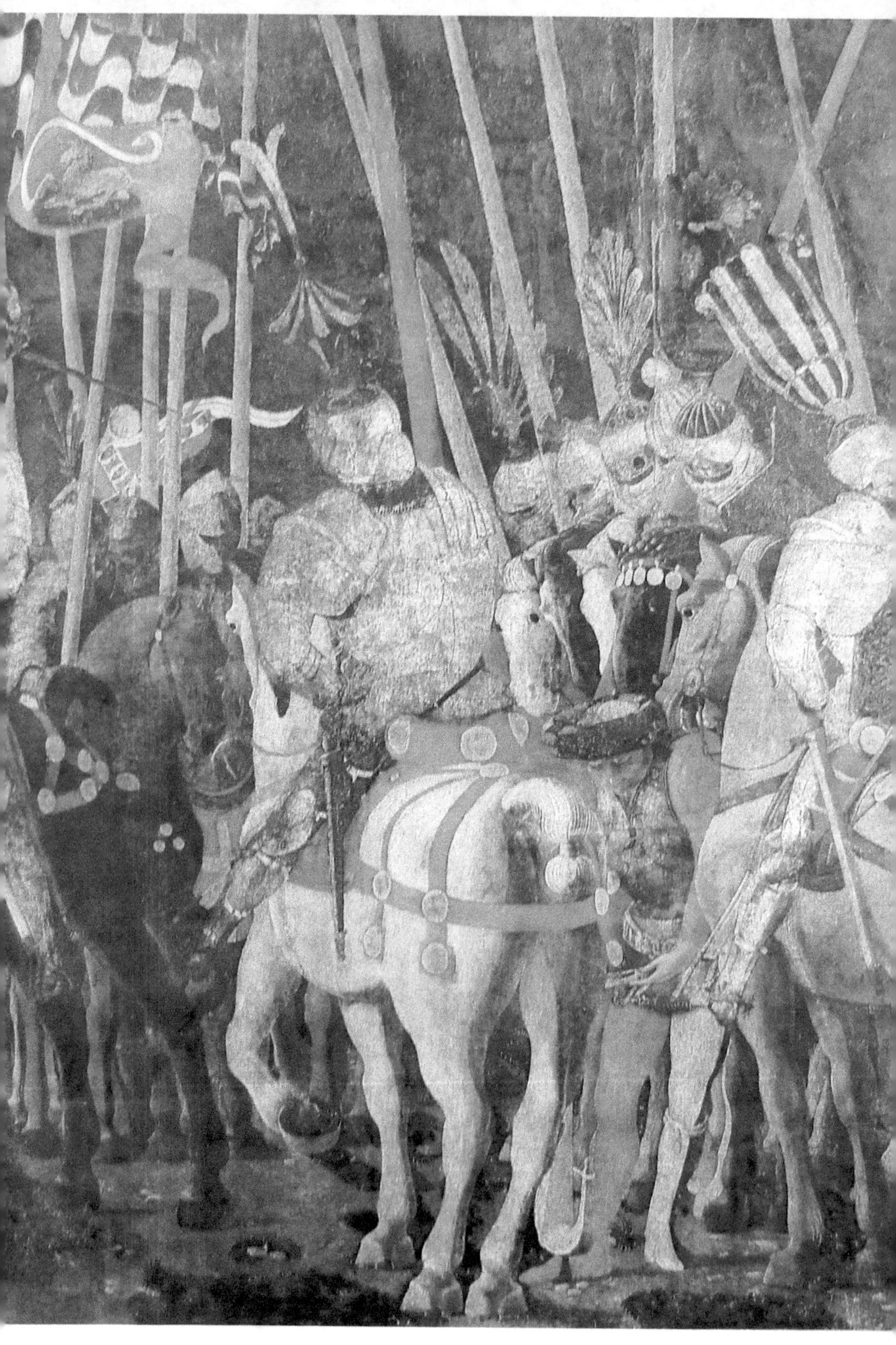

Paolo Uccello, The Battle of San Romano, Paris

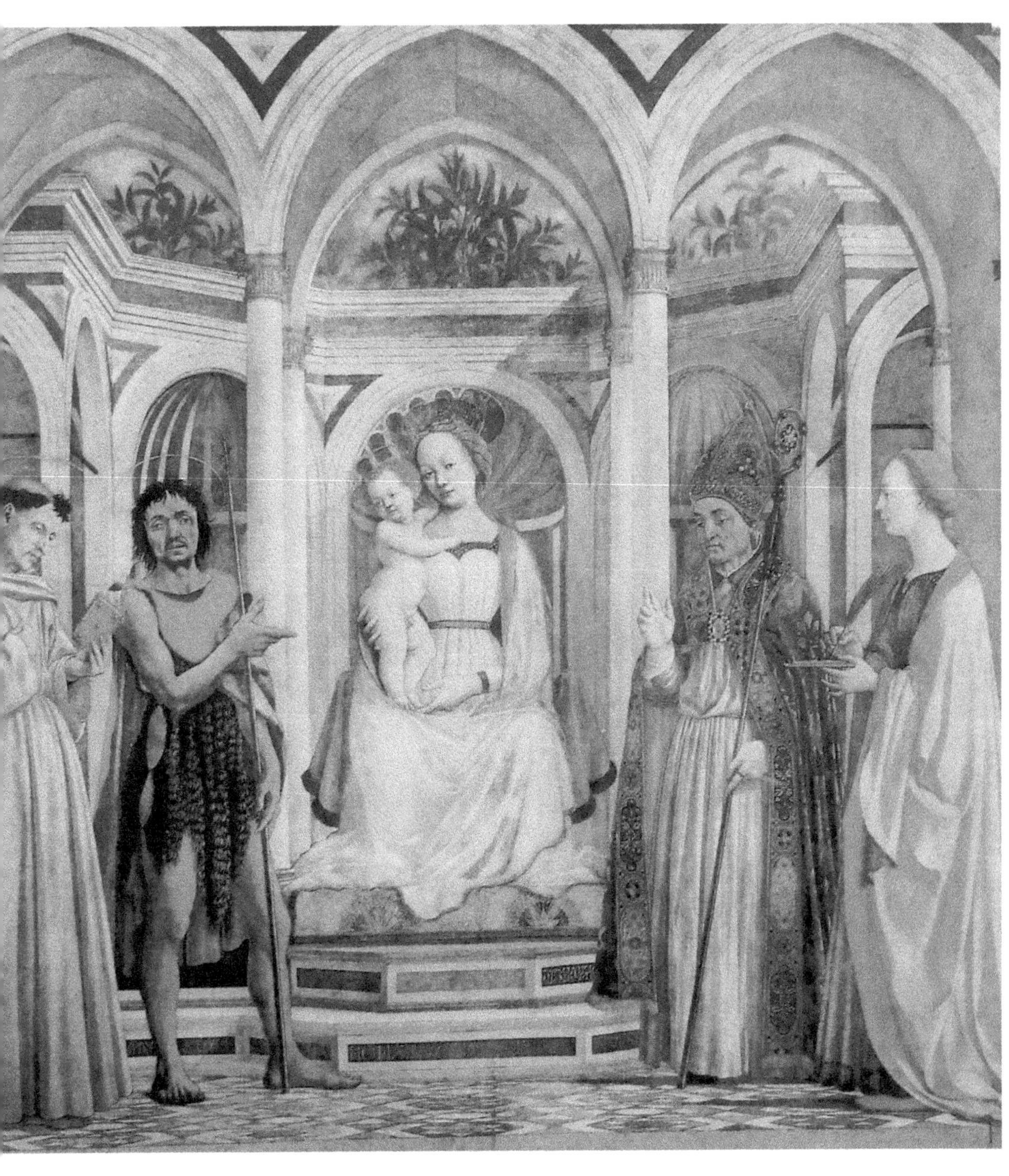

Domenico Veneziano, Madonna and Child With Saints, 1445, Uffizi Gallery

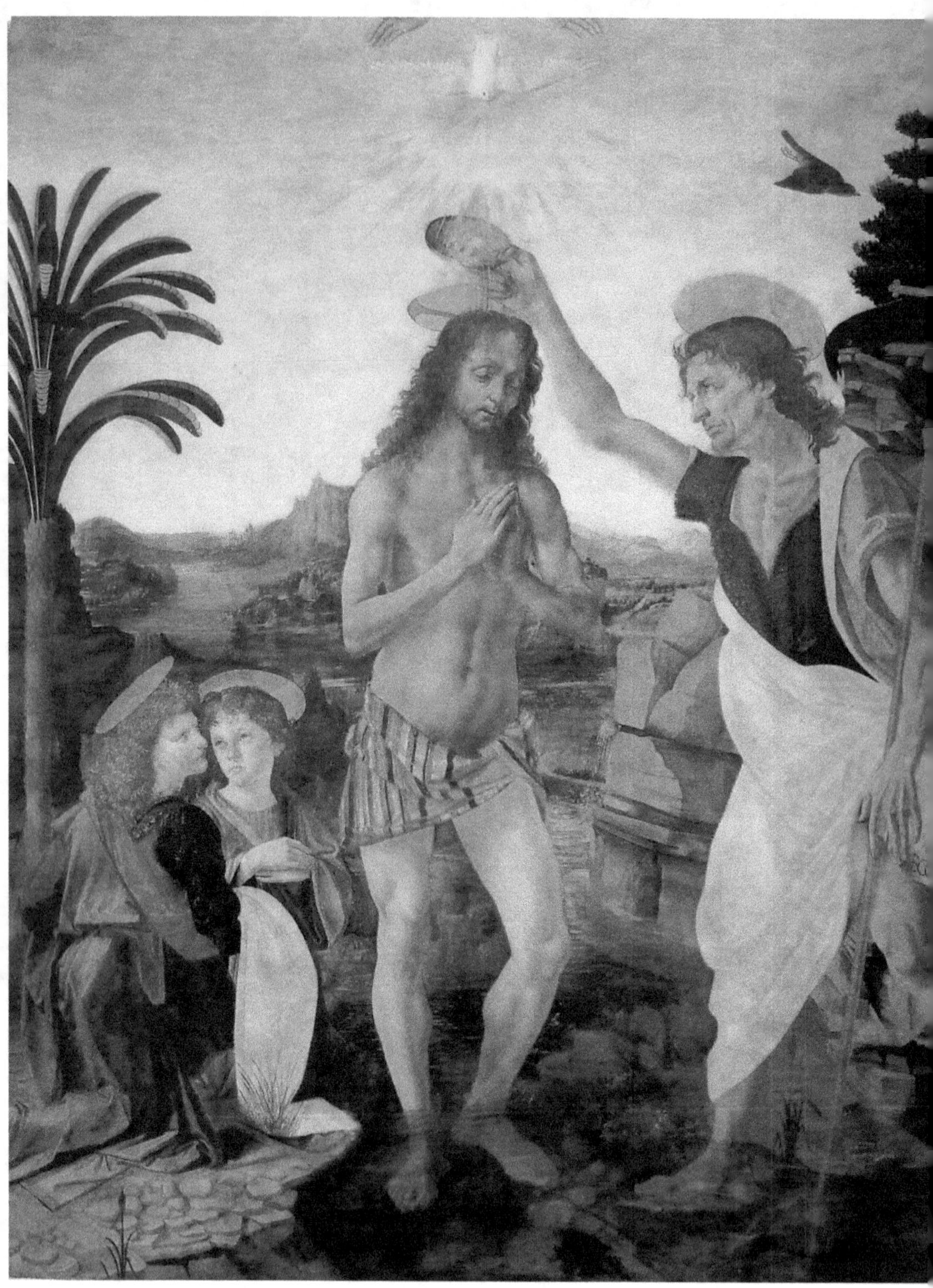

Andrea del Verrocchio, The Baptism of Christ

NOTES ON WORKS

THE VIRGIN ADORING THE INFANT SAVIOUR
(In the Accademia, Florence)

In this earliest known picture by Filippo Lippi, the painter is still entirely under the influence of his youthful training. It is just like an illuminated miniature on a large scale, and is lacking in unity of design or pictorial vision. Note the way in which the figure of the Madonna is detached from the background, without having any real plastic life; and how awkwardly the monk is placed in the corner. The rocky landscape, with its steep perspective, is still quite in the spirit of the early primitives, although certain realistic details, like the cut-down tree-stump behind the Virgin, and the reflection of the sky in the water, show his loving observation of Nature. The picture was for a long time attributed to Masaccio's master, Masolino.

ST. JOHN THE BAPTIST WITH SIX OTHER SAINTS
(In the National Gallery, London)

The companion picture to the "Annunciation" lunette is the first rendering in Italian art of a Santa Conversatione in the open air. It is just an assembly of seven saints, without any real inner connection, the two pairs at the sides - SS. Francis and Lawrence on the left, and SS. Anthony and Peter Martyr on the right - being absorbed in their own doings and paying no attention to the blessing which St. John apparently bestows upon SS. Cosmas and Damianus, the patron saints of the Medici family. The little glimpse of a landscape background behind the marble bench affords evidence of Fra Filippo's close study of Nature even at that early period.

THE VISION OF ST. BERNARD
(In the National Gallery, London)

The Vision of St. Bernard, although at present the mere ghost of a picture from which almost every vestige of the original colour has faded away, is an important landmark in Fra Filippo's life, as it is one of the few works about which we have definite dates. It is mentioned by Vasari as being one of two pictures intended to be placed over doors in the Palazzo della Signoria, Florence. A contemporary record states, that on May 16, 1447, Fra Filippo received 40 lire for having painted "the figure of the Virgin and of St. Bernard." The companion picture, which represented the "Annunciation," has disappeared.

THE ANNUNCIATION
(In the National Gallery, London)

This charming lunette and its companion, "St. John the Baptist and Six Saints," were painted for the decoration of an apartment in the Riccardi Palace, by order of Cosimo de' Medici, whose crest – three feathers in a ring – is introduced in the stucco ornamentation of the balustrade. They were painted about 1438, towards the end of Fra Filippo's first Florentine period, and show far greater richness of colour and better management of light than his earlier known works at the Florence Academy. The perspective is still faulty, and the vase in the centre of the picture is terribly out of drawing. It has been suggested that this picture and the "Seven Saints" were the very panels on which Filippo Lippi was at work when he effected his romantic escape from Cosimo's palace, which is the subject of Browning's well-known poem.

THE CORONATION OF THE VIRGIN
(In the Accademia, Florence)

The crowning achievement of Filippo Lippi's second Florentine period, the great "Coronation of the Virgin," was commissioned by Francesco de Maringhi, chaplain to the nuns of Sant' Ambrogio, who died long before the completion of the picture, having provided in his will of July 28, 1441, for the manner in which settlement should be effected. Thus, in 1441, Filippo was already engaged upon this altarpiece, which he did not complete before 1447. On June 9 of that year he was paid the stipulated fee of 1200 lire. Although the picture has suffered considerably, it is even in its present condition one of the most entrancing creations of Florentine art. That the painter himself was proud of the result of his labours, may be gathered from the fact that he introduced his own portrait in a prominent position. In Borghini's *Riposo*, published in 1797, it is stated that the painter's name, "Frater Filippus," was then to be seen somewhere near the centre of the picture.

THE VIRGIN AND CHILD
(In the Pitti Palace, Florence)

Painted at Prato, soon after the abduction of Lucrezia Buti by the amorous monk, the central group of this *tondo* may be reasonably assumed to portray Lucrezia and Filippo Lippi. The incidents in the background, which have been a source of inspiration for many succeeding artists, including Raphael himself, who echoes the figure of the basket-carrying woman in his "Incendio del Borgo," depict the birth of Mary, and the meeting of St. Anne and Joachim. The motif of the Birth of the Virgin is in reality a convenient excuse for the painting of a charmingly rendered scene of Florentine domestic life. The distribution of light and the harmonising of the strong colour-notes are managed with consummate skill.

THE VIRGIN AND CHILD WITH TWO ANGELS
(In the Uffizi Gallery, Florence)

Painted for the chapel in Cosimo de' Medici's palace, this picture was transferred to the Uffizi Gallery from the Royal store-rooms in 1776. More, perhaps, than in any other work by the master, the whole arrangement of the picture and the management of the planes reveal the influence of the relief sculpture by Donatello and his followers. It is particularly akin in spirit to the art of Rossellino. The landscape seen through a window opening behind the heads of the Madonna and the Infant Saviour, as well as the laughing angel in the foreground, are entirely new conceptions in Florentine painting. That the picture must have been much admired by Filippo Lippi's contemporaries is proved by the innumerable slightly modified versions of it which were produced by the next generation of Florentine painters.

THE VIRGIN AND CHILD, WITH ANGELS AND TWO ABBOTS

(In the Louvre, Paris)

This altarpiece was commissioned in 1437 by the Company of Orsanmichele for the Barbadori Chapel in Santo Spirito. It is the picture referred to by Domenico Veneziano in a letter to Piero de' Medici, dated April 1, 1438, in which he says that by working day and night Fra Filippo could not finish it within five years, which was probably a correct estimate of the time actually taken. Even in its present state of deterioration this stately altarpiece, which shows how much Filippo had learnt from the study of Masaccio's Carmine frescoes, justifies the high praise bestowed upon it by Vasari. The two figures kneeling before the steps of the throne are St. Augustine on the right, and St. Fredianus on the left.

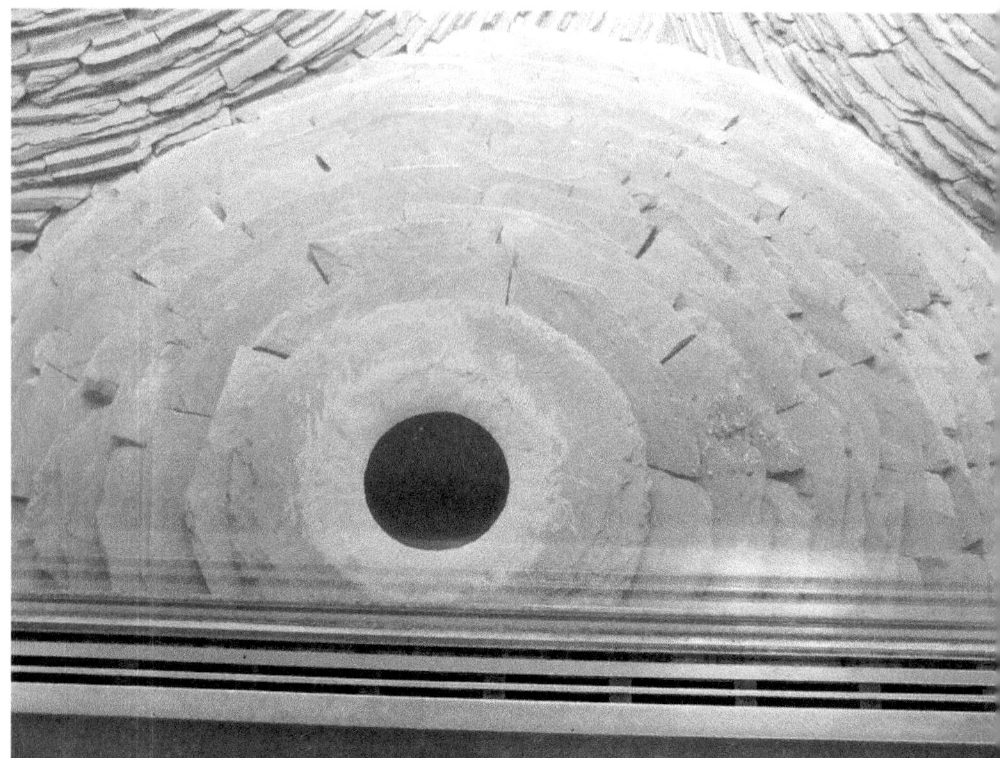

MAURICE SENDAK

& the art of children's book illustration

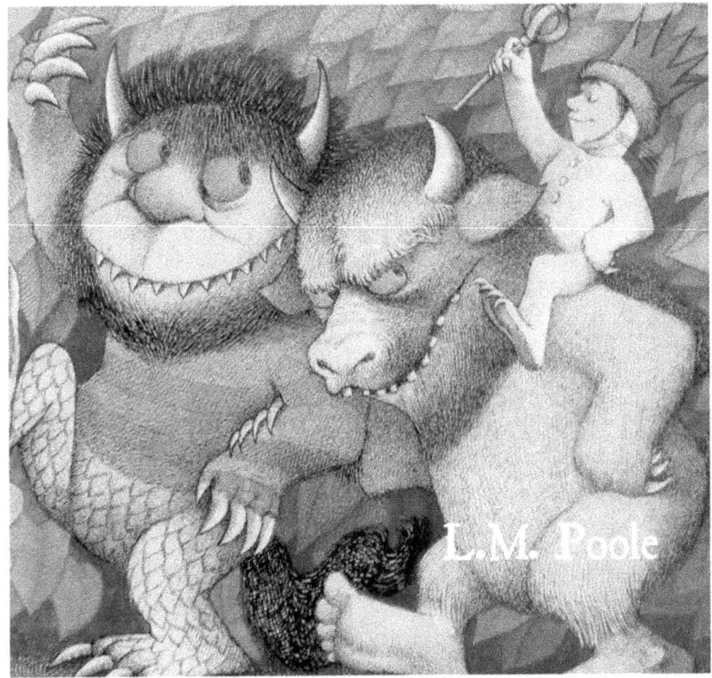

Maurice Sendak is the widely acclaimed American children's book author and illustrator. This critical study focuses on his famous trilogy, *Where the Wild Things Are*, *In the Night Kitchen* and *Outside Over There*, as well as the early works and Sendak's superb depictions of the Grimm Brothers' fairy tales in *The Juniper Tree*. L.M. Poole begins with a chapter on children's book illustration, in particular the treatment of fairy tales. Sendak's work is situated within the history of children's book illustration, and he is compared with many contemporary authors.

Fully illustrated. The book has been revised and updated for this edition.
ISBN 9781861714282 Pbk   ISBN 9781861713469 Hbk

CRESCENT MOON PUBLISHING

web: www.crmoon.com e-mail: cresmopub@yahoo.co.uk

ARTS, PAINTING, SCULPTURE

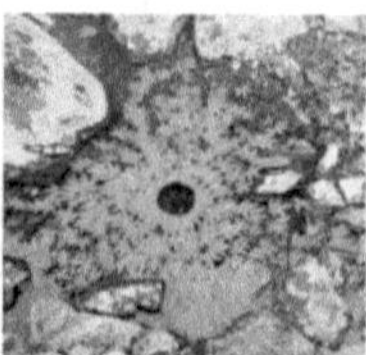

The Art of Andy Goldsworthy
Andy Goldsworthy: Touching Nature
Andy Goldsworthy in Close-Up
Andy Goldsworthy: Pocket Guide
Andy Goldsworthy In America
Land Art: A Complete Guide
The Art of Richard Long
Richard Long: Pocket Guide
Land Art In the UK
Land Art in Close-Up
Land Art In the U.S.A.
Land Art: Pocket Guide
Installation Art in Close-Up
Minimal Art and Artists In the 1960s and After
Colourfield Painting
Land Art DVD, TV documentary
Andy Goldsworthy DVD, TV documentary
The Erotic Object: Sexuality in Sculpture From Prehistory to the Present Day
Sex in Art: Pornography and Pleasure in Painting and Sculpture
Postwar Art
Sacred Gardens: The Garden in Myth, Religion and Art
Glorification: Religious Abstraction in Renaissance and 20th Century Art
Early Netherlandish Painting
Leonardo da Vinci
Piero della Francesca
Giovanni Bellini
Fra Angelico: Art and Religion in the Renaissance
Mark Rothko: The Art of Transcendence
Frank Stella: American Abstract Artist
Jasper Johns
Brice Marden
Alison Wilding: The Embrace of Sculpture
Vincent van Gogh: Visionary Landscapes
Eric Gill: Nuptials of God
Constantin Brancusi: Sculpting the Essence of Things
Max Beckmann
Caravaggio
Gustave Moreau
Egon Schiele: Sex and Death In Purple Stockings
Delizioso Fotografico Fervore: Works In Process 1
Sacro Cuore: Works In Process 2
The Light Eternal: J.M.W. Turner
The Madonna Glorified: Karen Arthurs

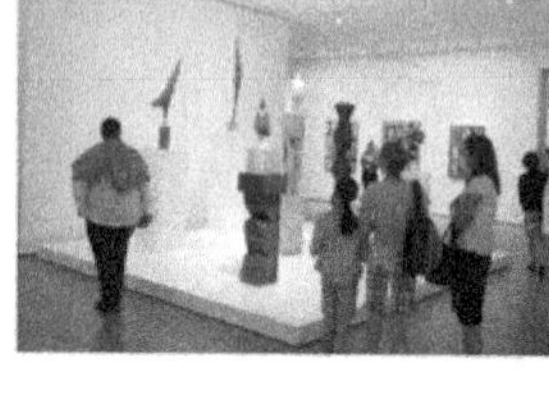

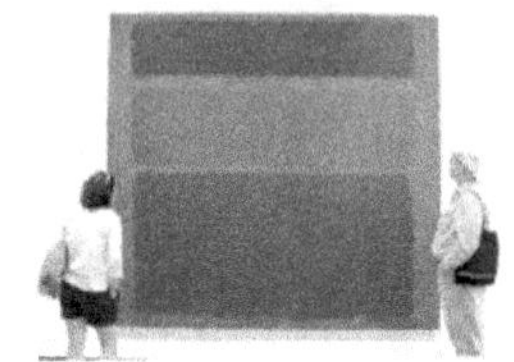

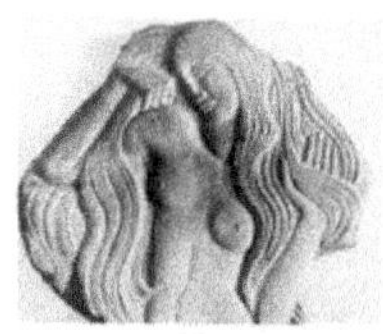

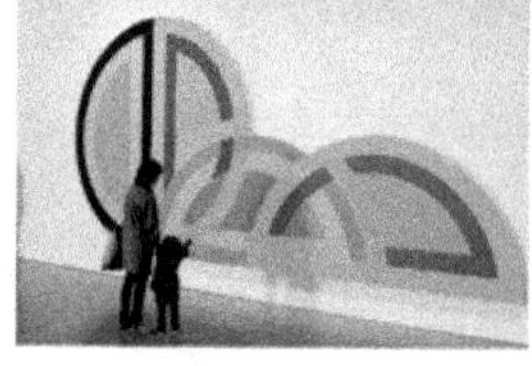

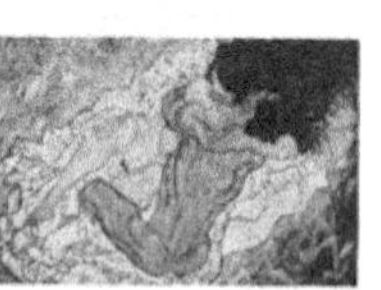

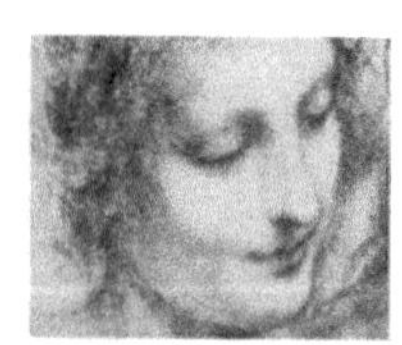

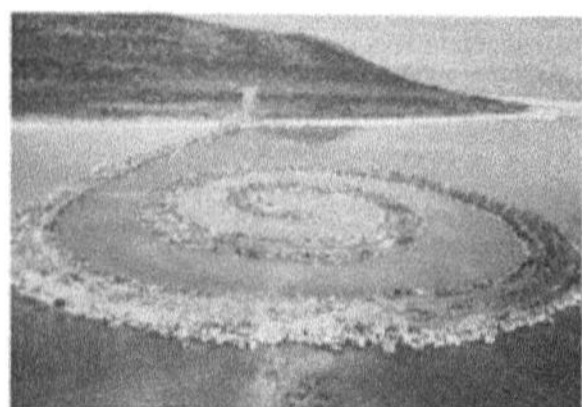

LITERATURE

J.R.R. Tolkien: The Books, The Films, The Whole Cultural Phenomenon
J.R.R. Tolkien: Pocket Guide
Tolkien's Heroic Quest
The *Earthsea* Books of Ursula Le Guin
Beauties, Beasts and Enchantment: Classic French Fairy Tales
German Popular Stories by the Brothers Grimm
Philip Pullman and *His Dark Materials*
Sexing Hardy: Thomas Hardy and Feminism
Thomas Hardy's *Tess of the d'Urbervilles*
Thomas Hardy's *Jude the Obscure*
Thomas Hardy: The Tragic Novels
Love and Tragedy: Thomas Hardy
The Poetry of Landscape in Hardy
Wessex Revisited: Thomas Hardy and John Cowper Powys
Wolfgang Iser: Essays and Interviews
Petrarch, Dante and the Troubadours
Maurice Sendak and the Art of Children's Book Illustration
Andrea Dworkin
Cixous, Irigaray, Kristeva: The *Jouissance* of French Feminism
Julia Kristeva: Art, Love, Melancholy, Philosophy, Semiotics and Psychoanalysis
Hélene Cixous I Love You: The *Jouissance* of Writing
Luce Irigaray: Lips, Kissing, and the Politics of Sexual Difference
Peter Redgrove: Here Comes the Flood
Peter Redgrove: Sex-Magic-Poetry-Cornwall
Lawrence Durrell: Between Love and Death, East and West
Love, Culture & Poetry: Lawrence Durrell
Cavafy: Anatomy of a Soul
German Romantic Poetry: Goethe, Novalis, Heine, Hölderlin
Feminism and Shakespeare
Shakespeare: Love, Poetry & Magic
The Passion of D.H. Lawrence
D.H. Lawrence: Symbolic Landscapes
D.H. Lawrence: Infinite Sensual Violence
Rimbaud: Arthur Rimbaud and the Magic of Poetry
The Ecstasies of John Cowper Powys
Sensualism and Mythology: The Wessex Novels of John Cowper Powys
Amorous Life: John Cowper Powys and the Manifestation of Affectivity (H.W. Fawkner)
Postmodern Powys: New Essays on John Cowper Powys (Joe Boulter)
Rethinking Powys: Critical Essays on John Cowper Powys
Paul Bowles & Bernardo Bertolucci
Rainer Maria Rilke
Joseph Conrad: *Heart of Darkness*
In the Dim Void: Samuel Beckett
Samuel Beckett Goes into the Silence
André Gide: Fiction and Fervour
Jackie Collins and the Blockbuster Novel
Blinded By Her Light: The Love-Poetry of Robert Graves
The Passion of Colours: Travels In Mediterranean Lands
Poetic Forms

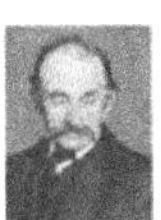
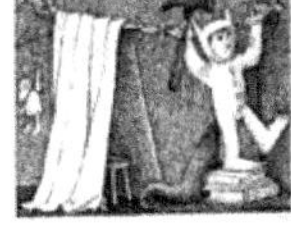
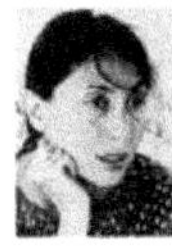
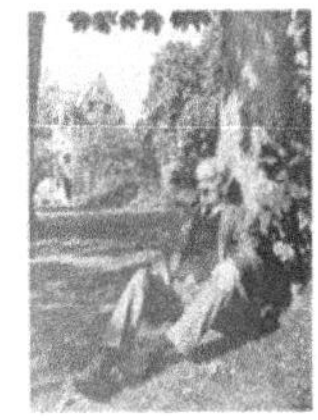
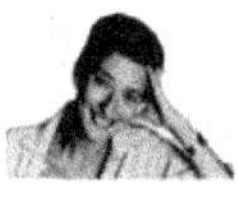
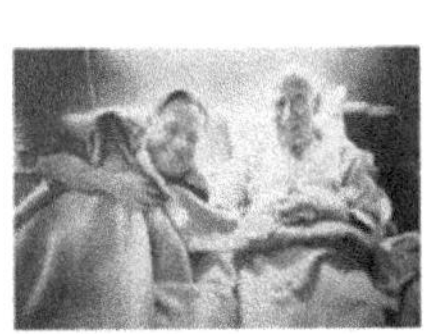
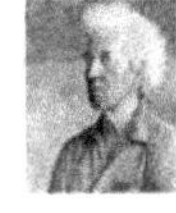
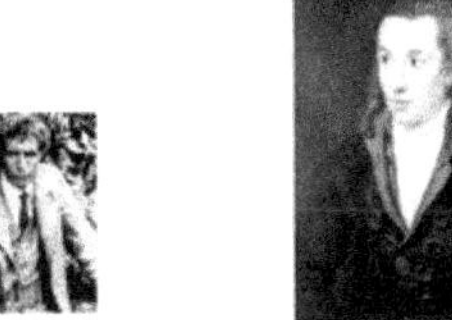

POETRY

Ursula Le Guin: Walking In Cornwall
Peter Redgrove: Here Comes The Flood
Peter Redgrove: Sex-Magic-Poetry-Cornwall
Dante: Selections From the Vita Nuova
Petrarch, Dante and the Troubadours
William Shakespeare: Sonnets
William Shakespeare: Complete Poems
Blinded By Her Light: The Love-Poetry of Robert Graves
Emily Dickinson: Selected Poems
Emily Brontë: Poems
Thomas Hardy: Selected Poems
Percy Bysshe Shelley: Poems
John Keats: Selected Poems
Joh n Keats: Poems of 1820
D.H. Lawrence: Selected Poems
Edmund Spenser: Poems
Edmund Spenser: Amoretti
John Donne: Poems
Henry Vaughan: Poems
Sir Thomas Wyatt: Poems
Robert Herrick: Selected Poems
Rilke: Space, Essence and Angels in the Poetry of Rainer Maria Rilke
Rainer Maria Rilke: Selected Poems
Friedrich Hölderlin: Selected Poems
Arseny Tarkovsky: Selected Poems
Arthur Rimbaud: Selected Poems
Arthur Rimbaud: A Season in Hell
Arthur Rimbaud and the Magic of Poetry
Novalis: Hymns To the Night
German Romantic Poetry
Paul Verlaine: Selected Poems
Elizaethan Sonnet Cycles
D.J. Enright: By-Blows
Jeremy Reed: Brigitte's Blue Heart
Jeremy Reed: Claudia Schiffer's Red Shoes
Gorgeous Little Orpheus
Radiance: New Poems
Crescent Moon Book of Nature Poetry
Crescent Moon Book of Love Poetry
Crescent Moon Book of Mystical Poetry
Crescent Moon Book of Elizabethan Love Poetry
Crescent Moon Book of Metaphysical Poetry
Crescent Moon Book of Romantic Poetry
Pagan America: New American Poetry

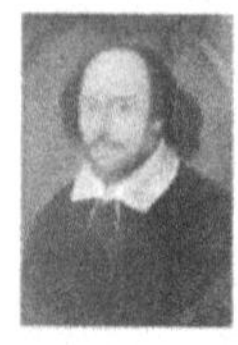
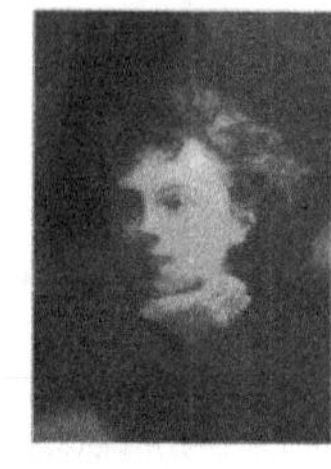
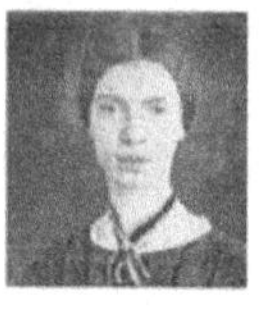
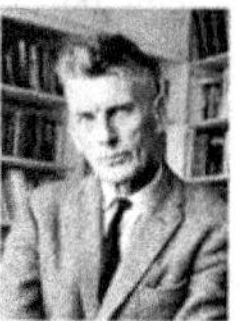
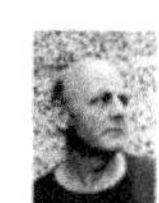
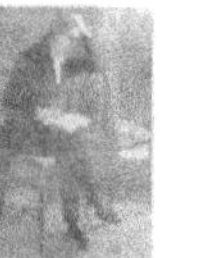
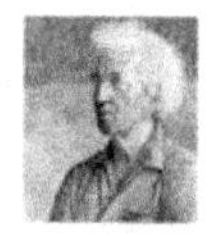
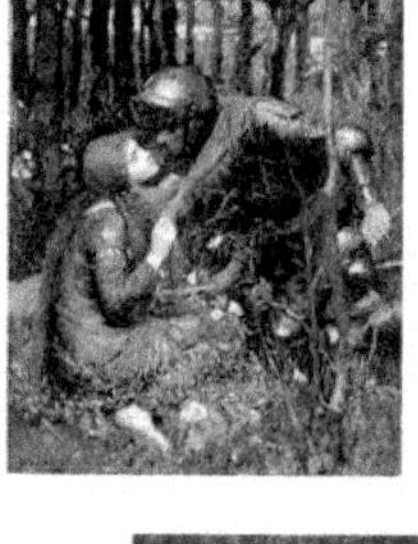
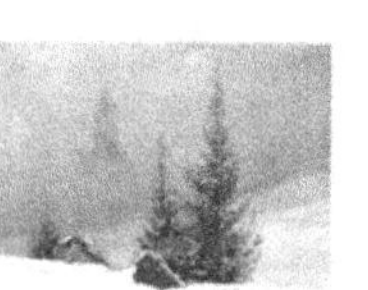
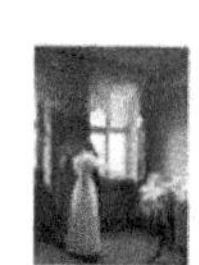
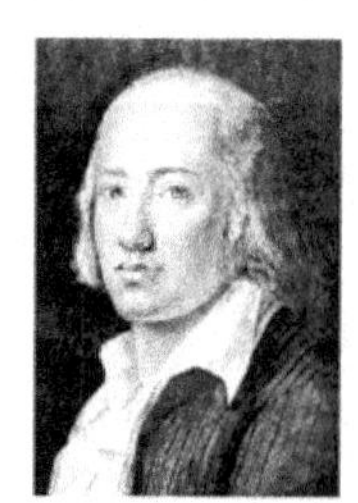
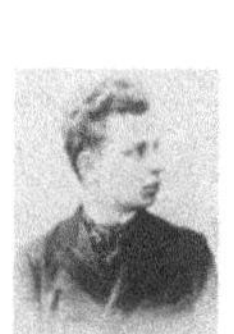
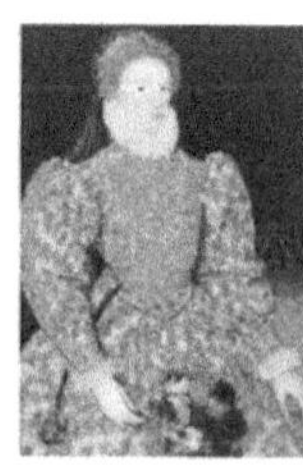

MEDIA, CINEMA, FEMINISM and CULTURAL STUDIES

J.R.R. Tolkien: The Books, The Films, The Whole Cultural Phenomenon
J.R.R. Tolkien: Pocket Guide
The *Lord of the Rings* Movies: Pocket Guide
The Cinema of Hayao Miyazaki
Hayao Miyazaki: *Princess Mononoke*: Pocket Movie Guide
Hayao Miyazaki: *Spirited Away*: Pocket Movie Guide
Tim Burton : Hallowe'en For Hollywood
Ken Russell

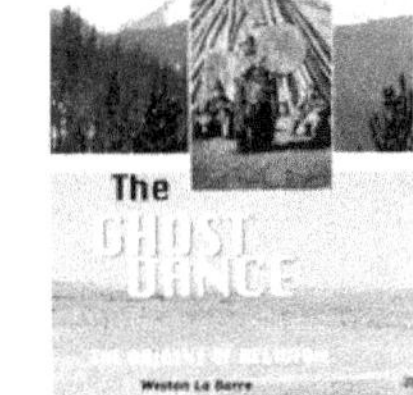

Ken Russell: *Tommy*: Pocket Movie Guide
The Ghost Dance: The Origins of Religion
The Peyote Cult
Cixous, Irigaray, Kristeva: The *Jouissance* of French Feminism
Julia Kristeva: Art, Love, Melancholy, Philosophy, Semiotics and Psychoanalysis
Luce Irigaray: Lips, Kissing, and the Politics of Sexual Difference
Hélene Cixous I Love You: The *Jouissance* of Writing
Andrea Dworkin

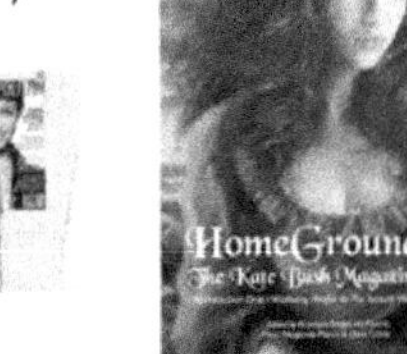

'Cosmo Woman': The World of Women's Magazines
Women in Pop Music
HomeGround: The Kate Bush Anthology
Discovering the Goddess (Geoffrey Ashe)
The Poetry of Cinema
The Sacred Cinema of Andrei Tarkovsky
Andrei Tarkovsky: Pocket Guide

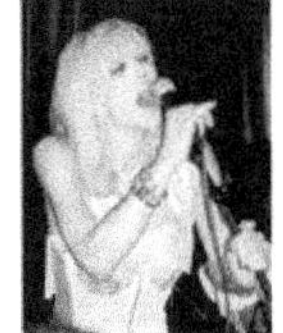

Andrei Tarkovsky: *Mirror*: Pocket Movie Guide
Andrei Tarkovsky: *The Sacrifice*: Pocket Movie Guide
Walerian Borowczyk: Cinema of Erotic Dreams
Jean-Luc Godard: The Passion of Cinema
Jean-Luc Godard: *Hail Mary*: Pocket Movie Guide
Jean-Luc Godard: *Contempt*: Pocket Movie Guide

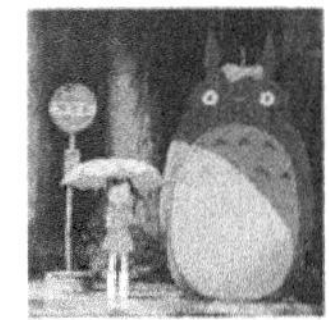

Jean-Luc Godard: *Pierrot le Fou*: Pocket Movie Guide

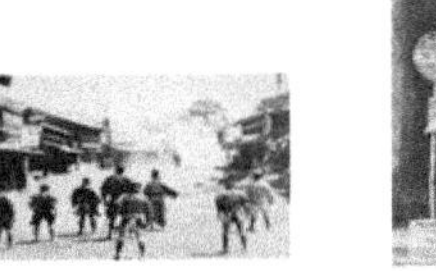

John Hughes and Eighties Cinema
Ferris Bueller's Day Off: Pocket Movie Guide
Jean-Luc Godard: Pocket Guide
The Cinema of Richard Linklater
Liv Tyler: Star In Ascendance
Blade Runner and the Films of Philip K. Dick

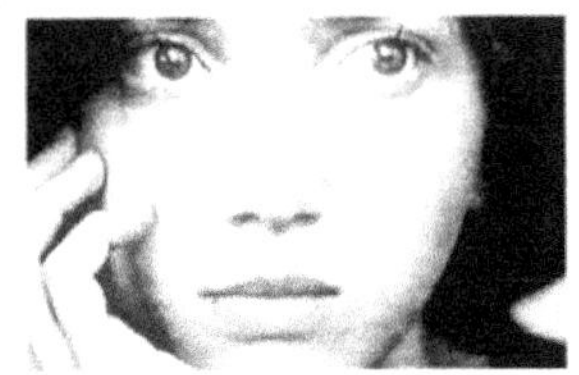

Paul Bowles and Bernardo Bertolucci
Media Hell: Radio, TV and the Press
An Open Letter to the BBC
Detonation Britain: Nuclear War in the UK
Feminism and Shakespeare
Wild Zones: Pornography, Art and Feminism
Sex in Art: Pornography and Pleasure in Painting and Sculpture
Sexing Hardy: Thomas Hardy and Feminism

The Light Eternal is a model monograph, an exemplary job. The subject matter of the book is beautifully organised and dead on beam. (Lawrence Durrell)

It is amazing for me to see my work treated with such passion and respect. (Andrea Dworkin)

CRESCENT MOON PUBLISHING
P.O. Box 1312, Maidstone, Kent, ME14 5XU, Great Britain. www.crmoon.com

cresmopub@yahoo.co.uk   www.crescentmoon.org.uk

www.ingramcontent.com/pod-product-compliance
Lightning Source LLC
LaVergne TN
LVHW020512100826
845148LV00003B/766

9781861717993

www.ingramcontent.com/pod-product-compliance
Lightning Source LLC
LaVergne TN
LVHW020512100826
845148LV00003B/766

* 9 7 8 1 8 6 1 7 1 7 9 9 3 *